MULTIPLICATION
AND DIVISION
PRACTICE PROBLEMS

ISBN: 1733837760
ISBN-13: 978-1733837767

Table of Contents

Part 1: Multiplication

Part 2: Division

Answer keys are provided at the back of the book.

Part 1
Multiplication

Assignment 1

Name _____   Score _____

1) 9
× 6

2) 7
× 3

3) 8
× 9

4) 5
× 5

5) 2
× 6

6) 9
× 4

7) 3
× 9

8) 6
× 5

9) 8
× 1

10) 9
× 2

11) 3
× 2

12) 8
× 6

13) 9
× 5

14) 2
× 5

15) 4
× 7

16) 4
× 3

17) 6
× 1

18) 7
× 7

19) 5
× 4

20) 8
× 2

Multiplication, 1 Digit × 1 Digit

Assignment 2

1)   7
   × 2

2)   6
   × 8

3)   8
   × 5

4)   3
   × 6

5)   2
   × 1

6)   5
   × 1

7)   4
   × 5

8)   2
   × 9

9)   4
   × 1

10)   3
    × 7

11)   9
    × 7

12)   8
    × 4

13)   7
    × 7

14)   8
    × 0

15)   5
    × 6

16)   3
    × 4

17)   1
    × 8

18)   2
    × 3

19)   7
    × 4

20)   8
    × 3

Multiplication, 1 Digit × 1 Digit

Assignment 3

1) $\begin{array}{r} 5 \\ \times\ 3 \\ \hline \end{array}$
2) $\begin{array}{r} 9 \\ \times\ 1 \\ \hline \end{array}$
3) $\begin{array}{r} 8 \\ \times\ 6 \\ \hline \end{array}$
4) $\begin{array}{r} 9 \\ \times\ 6 \\ \hline \end{array}$
5) $\begin{array}{r} 6 \\ \times\ 1 \\ \hline \end{array}$

6) $\begin{array}{r} 2 \\ \times\ 4 \\ \hline \end{array}$
7) $\begin{array}{r} 7 \\ \times\ 5 \\ \hline \end{array}$
8) $\begin{array}{r} 4 \\ \times\ 7 \\ \hline \end{array}$
9) $\begin{array}{r} 9 \\ \times\ 4 \\ \hline \end{array}$
10) $\begin{array}{r} 3 \\ \times\ 2 \\ \hline \end{array}$

11) $\begin{array}{r} 5 \\ \times\ 2 \\ \hline \end{array}$
12) $\begin{array}{r} 6 \\ \times\ 6 \\ \hline \end{array}$
13) $\begin{array}{r} 8 \\ \times\ 9 \\ \hline \end{array}$
14) $\begin{array}{r} 4 \\ \times\ 6 \\ \hline \end{array}$
15) $\begin{array}{r} 9 \\ \times\ 3 \\ \hline \end{array}$

16) $\begin{array}{r} 3 \\ \times\ 1 \\ \hline \end{array}$
17) $\begin{array}{r} 7 \\ \times\ 6 \\ \hline \end{array}$
18) $\begin{array}{r} 8 \\ \times\ 2 \\ \hline \end{array}$
19) $\begin{array}{r} 9 \\ \times\ 5 \\ \hline \end{array}$
20) $\begin{array}{r} 7 \\ \times\ 8 \\ \hline \end{array}$

Multiplication, 1 Digit × 1 Digit

Assignment 4

Name _____   Score _____

1) $6 \times \underline{\hspace{1cm}} = 42$

2) $8 \times \underline{\hspace{1cm}} = 8$

3) $9 \times \underline{\hspace{1cm}} = 45$

4) $7 \times \underline{\hspace{1cm}} = 14$

5) $1 \times \underline{\hspace{1cm}} = 3$

6) $2 \times \underline{\hspace{1cm}} = 10$

7) $6 \times \underline{\hspace{1cm}} = 48$

8) $6 \times \underline{\hspace{1cm}} = 36$

9) $5 \times \underline{\hspace{1cm}} = 15$

10) $4 \times \underline{\hspace{1cm}} = 8$

11) $8 \times \underline{\hspace{1cm}} = 24$

12) $3 \times \underline{\hspace{1cm}} = 21$

13) $6 \times \underline{\hspace{1cm}} = 54$

14) $2 \times \underline{\hspace{1cm}} = 6$

15) $9 \times \underline{\hspace{1cm}} = 36$

16) $4 \times \underline{\hspace{1cm}} = 20$

17) $8 \times \underline{\hspace{1cm}} = 64$

18) $7 \times \underline{\hspace{1cm}} = 28$

19) $4 \times \underline{\hspace{1cm}} = 12$

20) $8 \times \underline{\hspace{1cm}} = 56$

Find the missing number, 1 Digit × 1 Digit

Assignment 5

Name _____   Score _____

1) $\begin{array}{r} 7 \\ \times\ 4 \\ \hline \end{array}$	2) $\begin{array}{r} 3 \\ \times\ 3 \\ \hline \end{array}$	3) $\begin{array}{r} 7 \\ \times\ 8 \\ \hline \end{array}$	4) $\begin{array}{r} 9 \\ \times\ 4 \\ \hline \end{array}$	5) $\begin{array}{r} 2 \\ \times\ 3 \\ \hline \end{array}$	6) $\begin{array}{r} 8 \\ \times\ 3 \\ \hline \end{array}$
7) $\begin{array}{r} 5 \\ \times\ 9 \\ \hline \end{array}$	8) $\begin{array}{r} 1 \\ \times\ 2 \\ \hline \end{array}$	9) $\begin{array}{r} 9 \\ \times\ 0 \\ \hline \end{array}$	10) $\begin{array}{r} 4 \\ \times\ 6 \\ \hline \end{array}$	11) $\begin{array}{r} 5 \\ \times\ 8 \\ \hline \end{array}$	12) $\begin{array}{r} 6 \\ \times\ 6 \\ \hline \end{array}$
13) $\begin{array}{r} 8 \\ \times\ 9 \\ \hline \end{array}$	14) $\begin{array}{r} 6 \\ \times\ 7 \\ \hline \end{array}$	15) $\begin{array}{r} 2 \\ \times\ 2 \\ \hline \end{array}$	16) $\begin{array}{r} 3 \\ \times\ 4 \\ \hline \end{array}$	17) $\begin{array}{r} 7 \\ \times\ 9 \\ \hline \end{array}$	18) $\begin{array}{r} 7 \\ \times\ 5 \\ \hline \end{array}$
19) $\begin{array}{r} 6 \\ \times\ 8 \\ \hline \end{array}$	20) $\begin{array}{r} 2 \\ \times\ 9 \\ \hline \end{array}$	21) $\begin{array}{r} 1 \\ \times\ 3 \\ \hline \end{array}$	22) $\begin{array}{r} 8 \\ \times\ 0 \\ \hline \end{array}$	23) $\begin{array}{r} 4 \\ \times\ 7 \\ \hline \end{array}$	24) $\begin{array}{r} 3 \\ \times\ 5 \\ \hline \end{array}$
25) $\begin{array}{r} 1 \\ \times\ 7 \\ \hline \end{array}$	26) $\begin{array}{r} 6 \\ \times\ 2 \\ \hline \end{array}$	27) $\begin{array}{r} 6 \\ \times\ 9 \\ \hline \end{array}$	28) $\begin{array}{r} 7 \\ \times\ 7 \\ \hline \end{array}$	29) $\begin{array}{r} 2 \\ \times\ 4 \\ \hline \end{array}$	30) $\begin{array}{r} 1 \\ \times\ 9 \\ \hline \end{array}$
31) $\begin{array}{r} 2 \\ \times\ 5 \\ \hline \end{array}$	32) $\begin{array}{r} 8 \\ \times\ 8 \\ \hline \end{array}$	33) $\begin{array}{r} 3 \\ \times\ 6 \\ \hline \end{array}$	34) $\begin{array}{r} 1 \\ \times\ 4 \\ \hline \end{array}$	35) $\begin{array}{r} 5 \\ \times\ 7 \\ \hline \end{array}$	36) $\begin{array}{r} 4 \\ \times\ 8 \\ \hline \end{array}$
37) $\begin{array}{r} 4 \\ \times\ 4 \\ \hline \end{array}$	38) $\begin{array}{r} 3 \\ \times\ 1 \\ \hline \end{array}$	39) $\begin{array}{r} 5 \\ \times\ 4 \\ \hline \end{array}$	40) $\begin{array}{r} 3 \\ \times\ 7 \\ \hline \end{array}$	41) $\begin{array}{r} 9 \\ \times\ 6 \\ \hline \end{array}$	42) $\begin{array}{r} 5 \\ \times\ 4 \\ \hline \end{array}$
43) $\begin{array}{r} 3 \\ \times\ 8 \\ \hline \end{array}$	44) $\begin{array}{r} 2 \\ \times\ 6 \\ \hline \end{array}$	45) $\begin{array}{r} 9 \\ \times\ 9 \\ \hline \end{array}$	46) $\begin{array}{r} 9 \\ \times\ 2 \\ \hline \end{array}$	47) $\begin{array}{r} 1 \\ \times\ 5 \\ \hline \end{array}$	48) $\begin{array}{r} 8 \\ \times\ 4 \\ \hline \end{array}$
49) $\begin{array}{r} 1 \\ \times\ 8 \\ \hline \end{array}$	50) $\begin{array}{r} 5 \\ \times\ 5 \\ \hline \end{array}$	51) $\begin{array}{r} 6 \\ \times\ 4 \\ \hline \end{array}$	52) $\begin{array}{r} 2 \\ \times\ 7 \\ \hline \end{array}$	53) $\begin{array}{r} 4 \\ \times\ 9 \\ \hline \end{array}$	54) $\begin{array}{r} 5 \\ \times\ 0 \\ \hline \end{array}$
55) $\begin{array}{r} 9 \\ \times\ 5 \\ \hline \end{array}$	56) $\begin{array}{r} 1 \\ \times\ 6 \\ \hline \end{array}$	57) $\begin{array}{r} 3 \\ \times\ 9 \\ \hline \end{array}$	58) $\begin{array}{r} 5 \\ \times\ 6 \\ \hline \end{array}$	59) $\begin{array}{r} 4 \\ \times\ 3 \\ \hline \end{array}$	60) $\begin{array}{r} 2 \\ \times\ 8 \\ \hline \end{array}$

Assignment 6

Name _____   Score _____

1)   85
   × 3

2)   47
   × 4

3)   68
   × 9

4)   75
   × 5

5)   12
   × 6

6)   59
   × 4

7)   73
   × 9

8)   26
   × 5

9)   68
   × 3

10)   79
    × 2

11)   33
    × 2

12)   68
    × 6

13)   99
    × 3

14)   21
    × 5

15)   45
    × 7

16)   64
    × 3

17)   36
    × 2

18)   97
    × 7

19)   15
    × 4

20)   29
    × 6

Multiplication, 2 Digits × 1 Digit

Assignment 7

Name _____   Score _____

1)   27
   × 2

2)   56
   × 8

3)   78
   × 5

4)   93
   × 6

5)   12
   × 3

6)   35
   × 4

7)   64
   × 5

8)   92
   × 9

9)   42
   × 1

10)   53
   × 7

11)   79
   × 7

12)   98
   × 4

13)   17
   × 7

14)   38
   × 3

15)   45
   × 6

16)   23
   × 4

17)   71
   × 8

18)   26
   × 3

19)   87
   × 4

20)   38
   × 3

Assignment 8

Name _____   Score _____

1) $\begin{array}{r} 75 \\ \times\ 3 \\ \hline \end{array}$
2) $\begin{array}{r} 49 \\ \times\ 4 \\ \hline \end{array}$
3) $\begin{array}{r} 18 \\ \times\ 6 \\ \hline \end{array}$
4) $\begin{array}{r} 89 \\ \times\ 5 \\ \hline \end{array}$
5) $\begin{array}{r} 56 \\ \times\ 2 \\ \hline \end{array}$

6) $\begin{array}{r} 42 \\ \times\ 3 \\ \hline \end{array}$
7) $\begin{array}{r} 27 \\ \times\ 5 \\ \hline \end{array}$
8) $\begin{array}{r} 64 \\ \times\ 7 \\ \hline \end{array}$
9) $\begin{array}{r} 39 \\ \times\ 4 \\ \hline \end{array}$
10) $\begin{array}{r} 54 \\ \times\ 2 \\ \hline \end{array}$

11) $\begin{array}{r} 85 \\ \times\ 8 \\ \hline \end{array}$
12) $\begin{array}{r} 66 \\ \times\ 6 \\ \hline \end{array}$
13) $\begin{array}{r} 48 \\ \times\ 9 \\ \hline \end{array}$
14) $\begin{array}{r} 24 \\ \times\ 6 \\ \hline \end{array}$
15) $\begin{array}{r} 19 \\ \times\ 3 \\ \hline \end{array}$

16) $\begin{array}{r} 73 \\ \times\ 6 \\ \hline \end{array}$
17) $\begin{array}{r} 57 \\ \times\ 4 \\ \hline \end{array}$
18) $\begin{array}{r} 35 \\ \times\ 2 \\ \hline \end{array}$
19) $\begin{array}{r} 84 \\ \times\ 5 \\ \hline \end{array}$
20) $\begin{array}{r} 43 \\ \times\ 8 \\ \hline \end{array}$

Assignment 9

1) $74 \times$ _____ $= 148$

2) $36 \times$ _____ $= 180$

3) $58 \times$ _____ $= 464$

4) $66 \times$ _____ $= 264$

5) $24 \times$ _____ $= 168$

6) $53 \times$ _____ $= 318$

7) $76 \times$ _____ $= 608$

8) $25 \times$ _____ $= 100$

9) $62 \times$ _____ $= 186$

10) $77 \times$ _____ $= 231$

11) $34 \times$ _____ $= 238$

12) $67 \times$ _____ $= 335$

13) $96 \times$ _____ $= 192$

14) $23 \times$ _____ $= 138$

15) $48 \times$ _____ $= 96$

16) $62 \times$ _____ $= 372$

17) $37 \times$ _____ $= 148$

18) $95 \times$ _____ $= 665$

19) $13 \times$ _____ $= 26$

20) $21 \times$ _____ $= 63$

Find the missing number, 2 Digits × 1 Digit

Assignment 10

Name _____   **Score** _____

1) **24** × **6**	2) **43** × **5**	3) **67** × **8**	4) **81** × **5**	5) **17** × **9**	6) **32** × **2**
7) **53** × **1**	8) **74** × **7**	9) **89** × **9**	10) **11** × **8**	11) **34** × **3**	12) **63** × **4**
13) **84** × **4**	14) **16** × **7**	15) **92** × **0**	16) **78** × **9**	17) **52** × **9**	18) **36** × **6**
19) **62** × **7**	20) **88** × **4**	21) **45** × **6**	22) **19** × **8**	23) **31** × **2**	24) **76** × **8**
25) **47** × **5**	26) **22** × **3**	27) **54** × **8**	28) **75** × **5**	29) **86** × **7**	30) **12** × **4**
31) **33** × **5**	32) **51** × **4**	33) **73** × **3**	34) **96** × **4**	35) **46** × **7**	36) **79** × **6**
37) **61** × **7**	38) **85** × **5**	39) **97** × **3**	40) **42** × **6**	41) **21** × **8**	42) **35** × **8**
43) **44** × **9**	44) **72** × **9**	45) **93** × **2**	46) **15** × **4**	47) **39** × **2**	48) **64** × **6**
49) **23** × **5**	50) **41** × **8**	51) **71** × **3**	52) **38** × **5**	53) **18** × **7**	54) **98** × **4**
55) **65** × **9**	56) **37** × **2**	57) **48** × **9**	58) **83** × **4**	59) **28** × **9**	60) **57** × **6**

Assignment 11

Name _____   Score _____

1)   **185**   2)   **347**   3)   **568**   4)   **775**   5)   **812**
   × 5   **× 2**   **× 8**   **× 6**   **× 9**

6)   **259**   7)   **473**   8)   **626**   9)   **968**   10) **179**
   × 4   **× 7**   **× 5**   **× 3**   **× 2**

11) **433**   12) **368**   13) **799**   14) **521**   15) **645**
   × 2   **× 6**   **× 2**   **× 5**   **× 7**

16) **964**   17) **636**   18) **397**   19) **115**   20) **829**
   × 3   **× 2**   **× 7**   **× 4**   **× 6**

Multiplication, 3 Digits × 1 Digit

Assignment 12

Name _____   Score _____

1)   427
  ×   8

2)   156
  ×   2

3)   778
  ×   5

4)   893
  ×   6

5)   312
  ×   3

6)   235
  ×   4

7)   564
  ×   5

8)   892
  ×   9

9)   442
  ×   1

10)   153
  ×   7

11)   279
  ×   7

12)   598
  ×   4

13)   817
  ×   7

14)   738
  ×   3

15)   645
  ×   6

16)   423
  ×   4

17)   971
  ×   8

18)   526
  ×   3

19)   387
  ×   4

20)   738
  ×   3

Assignment 13

Name _____   Score _____

1)   875
     ×   6

2)   249
     ×   4

3)   618
     ×   3

4)   389
     ×   5

5)   156
     ×   2

6)   742
     ×   3

7)   427
     ×   5

8)   564
     ×   7

9)   939
     ×   4

10)   254
     ×   2

11)   185
     ×   2

12)   466
     ×   6

13)   648
     ×   9

14)   824
     ×   6

15)   519
     ×   3

16)   373
     ×   6

17)   657
     ×   6

18)   948
     ×   2

19)   184
     ×   5

20)   243
     ×   8

Multiplication, 3 Digits × 1 Digit

Assignment 14

Name _____   Score _____

1) $316 \times$ _____ $= 632$

2) $938 \times$ _____ $= 7{,}504$

3) $559 \times$ _____ $= 3{,}354$

4) $467 \times$ _____ $= 1{,}868$

5) $681 \times$ _____ $= 3{,}405$

6) $742 \times$ _____ $= 3{,}710$

7) $176 \times$ _____ $= 1{,}408$

8) $296 \times$ _____ $= 1{,}776$

9) $815 \times$ _____ $= 2{,}445$

10) $434 \times$ _____ $= 868$

11) $578 \times$ _____ $= 1{,}734$

12) $793 \times$ _____ $= 5{,}551$

13) $946 \times$ _____ $= 8{,}514$

14) $652 \times$ _____ $= 1{,}956$

15) $129 \times$ _____ $= 516$

16) $234 \times$ _____ $= 1{,}170$

17) $468 \times$ _____ $= 3{,}744$

18) $687 \times$ _____ $= 2{,}748$

19) $912 \times$ _____ $= 5{,}472$

20) $818 \times$ _____ $= 5{,}726$

Assignment 15

Name _____   Score _____

1) 324 ×5	2) 143 ×6	3) 568 ×7	4) 881 ×9	5) 217 ×9	6) 432 ×2
7) 753 ×7	8) 474 ×1	9) 289 ×9	10) 311 ×8	11) 934 ×3	12) 863 ×4
13) 484 ×4	14) 316 ×7	15) 892 ×2	16) 578 ×9	17) 542 ×9	18) 336 ×6
19) 612 ×7	20) 848 ×4	21) 465 ×8	22) 199 ×6	23) 301 ×2	24) 736 ×8
25) 470 ×5	26) 223 ×3	27) 546 ×8	28) 758 ×5	29) 864 ×7	30) 124 ×4
31) 335 ×5	32) 510 ×4	33) 734 ×3	34) 965 ×7	35) 468 ×4	36) 796 ×6
37) 261 ×7	38) 485 ×4	39) 697 ×6	40) 942 ×3	41) 121 ×8	42) 305 ×8
43) 744 ×9	44) 572 ×9	45) 393 ×2	46) 115 ×4	47) 939 ×2	48) 764 ×6
49) 423 ×5	50) 641 ×8	51) 871 ×3	52) 538 ×5	53) 108 ×7	54) 498 ×4
55) 365 ×9	56) 237 ×2	57) 648 ×4	58) 783 ×9	59) 528 ×9	60) 947 ×6

Assignment 16

Name _____   Score _____

1) 1,385
× 9

2) 5,347
× 6

3) 4,687
× 8

4) 7,075
× 2

5) 8,212
× 5

6) 2,159
× 2

7) 3,473
× 3

8) 6,526
× 5

9) 9,608
× 7

10) 4,179
× 4

11) 7,433
× 7

12) 3,268
× 5

13) 7,949
× 2

14) 4,521
× 6

15) 1,645
× 2

16) 9,964
× 6

17) 4,636
× 4

18) 2,397
× 7

19) 3,115
× 2

20) 8,029
× 3

Multiplication, 4 Digits × 1 Digit

Assignment 17

Name _____   Score _____

1) **2,427**
× **3**

2) **3,156**
× **6**

3) **7,078**
× **5**

4) **8,493**
× **2**

5) **5,312**
× **8**

6) **1,235**
× **7**

7) **5,164**
× **1**

8) **8,292**
× **9**

9) **4,342**
× **5**

10) **3,153**
× **4**

11) **6,279**
× **6**

12) **8,598**
× **3**

13) **4,817**
× **7**

14) **7,238**
× **4**

15) **1,645**
× **7**

16) **2,423**
× **3**

17) **9,701**
× **4**

18) **5,426**
× **3**

19) **3,287**
× **8**

20) **7,383**
× **5**

Multiplication, 4 Digits × 1 Digit

Assignment 18

Name _____   **Score** _____

1) $1,875$
   $\times \quad 2$

2) $4,249$
   $\times \quad 5$

3) $6,183$
   $\times \quad 3$

4) $3,809$
   $\times \quad 4$

5) $9,156$
   $\times \quad 6$

6) $7,242$
   $\times \quad 2$

7) $4,275$
   $\times \quad 4$

8) $5,564$
   $\times \quad 7$

9) $8,939$
   $\times \quad 5$

10) $2,534$
    $\times \quad 3$

11) $1,850$
    $\times \quad 3$

12) $4,656$
    $\times \quad 6$

13) $6,248$
    $\times \quad 9$

14) $8,242$
    $\times \quad 5$

15) $5,319$
    $\times \quad 2$

16) $3,473$
    $\times \quad 8$

17) $6,576$
    $\times \quad 5$

18) $9,248$
    $\times \quad 2$

19) $4,184$
    $\times \quad 7$

20) $1,249$
    $\times \quad 6$

Multiplication, 4 Digits × 1 Digit

Assignment 19

Name _____   Score _____

1) $2{,}316 \times \underline{\hspace{1cm}} = 11{,}580$

2) $9{,}228 \times \underline{\hspace{1cm}} = 36{,}912$

3) $5{,}359 \times \underline{\hspace{1cm}} = 32{,}154$

4) $4{,}670 \times \underline{\hspace{1cm}} = 37{,}360$

5) $4{,}681 \times \underline{\hspace{1cm}} = 9{,}362$

6) $7{,}423 \times \underline{\hspace{1cm}} = 14{,}846$

7) $1{,}765 \times \underline{\hspace{1cm}} = 5{,}295$

8) $2{,}964 \times \underline{\hspace{1cm}} = 17{,}784$

9) $5{,}815 \times \underline{\hspace{1cm}} = 46{,}520$

10) $6{,}434 \times \underline{\hspace{1cm}} = 32{,}170$

11) $5{,}378 \times \underline{\hspace{1cm}} = 21{,}512$

12) $9{,}793 \times \underline{\hspace{1cm}} = 29{,}379$

13) $8{,}464 \times \underline{\hspace{1cm}} = 76{,}176$

14) $3{,}652 \times \underline{\hspace{1cm}} = 25{,}564$

15) $7{,}129 \times \underline{\hspace{1cm}} = 21{,}387$

16) $6{,}234 \times \underline{\hspace{1cm}} = 43{,}638$

17) $2{,}468 \times \underline{\hspace{1cm}} = 7{,}404$

18) $4{,}687 \times \underline{\hspace{1cm}} = 18{,}748$

19) $9{,}044 \times \underline{\hspace{1cm}} = 72{,}352$

20) $8{,}218 \times \underline{\hspace{1cm}} = 41{,}090$

Find the missing number, 4 Digits × 1 Digit

Assignment 20

Name _____   Score _____

1) 5,324
× 2

2) 3,143
× 8

3) 1,568
× 9

4) 8,981
× 7

5) 2,107
× 6

6) 4,158
× 5

7) 7,253
× 4

8) 4,574
× 3

9) 8,289
× 8

10) 5,311
× 9

11) 9,326
× 1

12) 8,063
× 7

13) 4,384
× 6

14) 7,316
× 9

15) 8,922
× 7

16) 5,978
× 2

17) 6,542
× 7

18) 3,236
× 4

19) 6,129
× 8

20) 8,348
× 2

21) 2,465
× 6

22) 7,199
× 8

23) 3,019
× 4

24) 8,736
× 7

25) 4,670
× 4

26) 3,223
× 7

27) 9,546
× 5

28) 7,587
× 8

29) 6,864
× 3

30) 5,124
× 5

31) 7,335
× 6

32) 5,104
× 4

33) 6,734
× 7

34) 9,265
× 3

35) 4,680
× 4

36) 8,796
× 5

37) 1,261
× 8

38) 4,853
× 5

39) 6,697
× 3

40) 5,942
× 6

41) 4,121
× 4

42) 3,058
× 7

43) 2,744
× 6

44) 5,372
× 2

45) 8,393
× 4

46) 9,115
× 2

47) 3,939
× 7

48) 7,642
× 9

49) 4,323
× 4

50) 6,411
× 7

51) 8,471
× 5

52) 1,538
× 3

53) 9,108
× 8

54) 5,498
× 5

55) 8,365
× 6

56) 7,237
× 7

57) 4,648
× 9

58) 1,783
× 4

59) 5,208
× 2

60) 3,587
× 9

Assignment 21

Name _____   Score _____

1)   **12**
  × 23

2)   **74**
  × 34

3)   **68**
  × 59

4)   **47**
  × 75

5)   **85**
  × 96

6)   **79**
  × 84

7)   **68**
  × 49

8)   **26**
  × 15

9)   **73**
  × 53

10)   **59**
  × 42

11)   **45**
  × 72

12)   **21**
  × 66

13)   **98**
  × 32

14)   **68**
  × 25

15)   **33**
  × 97

16)   **29**
  × 43

17)   **15**
  × 52

18)   **47**
  × 71

19)   **36**
  × 64

20)   **27**
  × 55

Assignment 22

Name _____   Score _____

1)   12
   × 42

2)   93
   × 68

3)   78
   × 65

4)   56
   × 26

5)   27
   × 53

6)   53
   × 64

7)   42
   × 75

8)   92
   × 39

9)   64
   × 21

10)   35
   × 47

11)   45
   × 57

12)   38
   × 14

13)   17
   × 87

14)   98
   × 63

15)   79
   × 46

16)   38
   × 24

17)   87
   × 48

18)   26
   × 53

19)   71
   × 94

20)   23
   × 73

Multiplication, 2 Digits × 2 Digits

Assignment 23

Name _____ **Score** _____

1) 56×39

2) 89×42

3) 18×63

4) 49×51

5) 75×27

6) 54×36

7) 39×56

8) 64×79

9) 27×41

10) 19×27

11) 19×22

12) 24×63

13) 48×95

14) 66×26

15) 85×38

16) 43×64

17) 84×26

18) 35×12

19) 57×59

20) 73×81

Multiplication, 2 Digits × 2 Digits

Assignment 24

Name _____   Score _____

1) 32 × 61	2) 17 × 52	3) 81 × 83	4) 67 × 48	5) 43 × 95	6) 24 × 27
7) 63 × 13	8) 34 × 75	9) 11 × 97	10) 89 × 82	11) 74 × 35	12) 53 × 47
13) 36 × 43	14) 52 × 79	15) 78 × 15	16) 92 × 39	17) 16 × 94	18) 84 × 62
19) 76 × 27	20) 31 × 43	21) 19 × 65	22) 45 × 89	23) 88 × 24	24) 62 × 83
25) 12 × 52	26) 86 × 35	27) 75 × 89	28) 54 × 26	29) 22 × 78	30) 47 × 42
31) 79 × 35	32) 46 × 24	33) 96 × 13	34) 73 × 84	35) 51 × 47	36) 33 × 56
37) 35 × 71	38) 21 × 52	39) 42 × 35	40) 97 × 46	41) 85 × 71	42) 61 × 68
43) 64 × 59	44) 39 × 96	45) 15 × 27	46) 93 × 45	47) 72 × 26	48) 44 × 63
49) 98 × 25	50) 18 × 48	51) 38 × 63	52) 71 × 85	53) 41 × 37	54) 23 × 54
55) 57 × 79	56) 28 × 52	57) 83 × 69	58) 48 × 47	59) 37 × 91	60) 65 × 16

Assignment 25

Name _____   Score _____

1) 285
× 31

2) 475
× 46

3) 686
× 98

4) 759
× 51

5) 125
× 63

6) 597
× 45

7) 734
× 91

8) 206
× 53

9) 689
× 38

10) 794
× 22

11) 338
× 25

12) 680
× 62

13) 993
× 34

14) 216
× 51

15) 453
× 79

16) 642
× 36

17) 236
× 42

18) 897
× 67

19) 415
× 24

20) 929
× 36

Multiplication, 3 Digits × 2 Digits

Assignment 26

Name _____   Score _____

1) 427
× 52

2) 856
× 68

3) 678
× 45

4) 793
× 59

5) 112
× 73

6) 535
× 94

7) 364
× 85

8) 692
× 49

9) 342
× 51

10) 453
× 67

11) 479
× 27

12) 298
× 64

13) 517
× 97

14) 438
× 83

15) 541
× 62

16) 203
× 47

17) 711
× 82

18) 263
× 35

19) 879
× 64

20) 387
× 35

Multiplication, 3 Digits × 2 Digits

Assignment 27

1) 752
× 34

2) 497
× 42

3) 183
× 69

4) 809
× 52

5) 563
× 27

6) 428
× 39

7) 271
× 25

8) 643
× 47

9) 395
× 46

10) 754
× 28

11) 850
× 29

12) 616
× 26

13) 483
× 49

14) 245
× 67

15) 198
× 39

16) 731
× 63

17) 575
× 47

18) 335
× 26

19) 842
× 51

20) 439
× 82

Assignment 28

Name _____   Score _____

1) 124
   × 62

2) 343
   × 54

3) 567
   × 86

4) 817
   × 58

5) 917
   × 91

6) 302
   × 25

7) 532
   × 31

8) 744
   × 57

9) 896
   × 79

10) 181
    × 98

11) 304
    × 31

12) 632
    × 34

13) 844
    × 54

14) 616
    × 79

15) 902
    × 13

16) 782
    × 39

17) 524
    × 95

18) 636
    × 76

19) 862
    × 82

20) 583
    × 14

21) 452
    × 63

22) 191
    × 83

23) 312
    × 28

24) 765
    × 84

25) 472
    × 43

26) 224
    × 36

27) 549
    × 76

28) 752
    × 53

29) 846
    × 75

30) 126
    × 84

31) 303
    × 59

32) 512
    × 43

33) 734
    × 32

34) 968
    × 49

35) 462
    × 73

36) 794
    × 65

37) 616
    × 78

38) 859
    × 51

39) 972
    × 34

40) 425
    × 76

41) 218
    × 81

42) 352
    × 38

43) 445
    × 96

44) 727
    × 81

45) 933
    × 24

46) 155
    × 46

47) 397
    × 28

48) 649
    × 61

49) 232
    × 53

50) 414
    × 85

51) 716
    × 37

52) 388
    × 59

53) 198
    × 71

54) 982
    × 43

55) 645
    × 95

56) 376
    × 27

57) 488
    × 91

58) 832
    × 43

59) 284
    × 96

60) 577
    × 62

Assignment 29

Name _____   Score _____

1) 2,185
 × 35

2) 4,347
 × 52

3) 6,568
 × 78

4) 9,775
 × 36

5) 1,812
 × 39

6) 3,259
 × 54

7) 7,473
 × 97

8) 1,626
 × 45

9) 5,968
 × 83

10) 9,179
 × 21

11) 4,303
 × 12

12) 2,368
 × 36

13) 4,799
 × 52

14) 6,521
 × 75

15) 8,645
 × 97

16) 1,964
 × 23

17) 3,636
 × 42

18) 6,397
 × 87

19) 9,115
 × 23

20) 3,829
 × 46

Assignment 30

1) 5,427
   ×   78

2) 7,156
   ×   92

3) 9,778
   ×   15

4) 8,093
   ×   26

5) 4,312
   ×   63

6) 8,235
   ×   94

7) 1,533
   ×   35

8) 4,892
   ×   69

9) 3,442
   ×   41

10) 5,153
    ×   37

11) 2,079
    ×   73

12) 5,981
    ×   45

13) 8,174
    ×   76

14) 7,387
    ×   31

15) 6,459
    ×   64

16) 1,526
    ×   52

17) 9,712
    ×   83

18) 5,264
    ×   35

19) 3,876
    ×   48

20) 7,224
    ×   31

Assignment 31

Name _____ Score _____

1) 8,752
× 63

2) 2,495
× 47

3) 6,182
× 39

4) 7,389
× 58

5) 9,156
× 21

6) 7,049
× 34

7) 4,329
× 58

8) 5,645
× 73

9) 9,309
× 44

10) 2,541
× 25

11) 1,856
× 27

12) 4,686
× 69

13) 6,408
× 91

14) 8,242
× 36

15) 5,194
× 35

16) 3,736
× 67

17) 6,578
× 96

18) 9,408
× 21

19) 1,842
× 53

20) 2,434
× 86

Assignment 32

Name _____   Score _____

1) 3,241
× 53

2) 1,434
× 67

3) 5,685
× 79

4) 8,801
× 31

5) 2,172
× 94

6) 4,325
× 26

7) 7,532
× 74

8) 4,741
× 13

9) 2,895
× 97

10) 3,116
× 88

11) 9,349
× 31

12) 8,632
× 45

13) 4,384
× 46

14) 3,167
× 71

15) 8,923
× 21

16) 5,784
× 92

17) 5,429
× 93

18) 3,366
× 64

19) 6,127
× 75

20) 8,483
× 46

21) 4,659
× 87

22) 1,990
× 62

23) 3,013
× 23

24) 7,362
× 84

25) 4,705
× 55

26) 2,234
× 36

27) 5,463
× 87

28) 7,586
× 58

29) 8,649
× 79

30) 1,248
× 41

31) 3,351
× 55

32) 5,103
× 46

33) 7,344
× 37

34) 9,656
× 79

35) 4,681
× 43

36) 7,962
× 64

37) 2,615
× 78

38) 4,856
× 49

39) 6,978
× 61

40) 9,422
× 35

41) 1,214
× 87

42) 3,057
× 81

43) 7,446
× 92

44) 5,724
× 39

45) 3,935
× 24

46) 1,157
× 46

47) 9,391
× 25

48) 7,647
× 69

49) 4,235
× 57

50) 6,413
× 89

51) 8,713
× 34

52) 5,389
× 55

53) 1,089
× 75

54) 4,986
× 42

55) 3,653
× 97

56) 2,375
× 24

57) 6,486
× 49

58) 7,835
× 97

59) 5,286
× 69

60) 5,874
× 62

Assignment 33

Name _____   Score _____

1)   85
   × 0.5

2)   47
   × 0.2

3)   68
   × 0.8

4)   76
   × 0.6

5)   12
   × 0.9

6)   24
   × 0.4

7)   47
   × 0.7

8)   61
   × 0.5

9)   96
   × 0.3

10)   17
   × 0.2

11)   33
   × 0.26

12)   68
   × 0.47

13)   99
   × 0.32

14)   21
   × 0.45

15)   45
   × 0.87

16)   64
   × 0.73

17)   36
   × 0.92

18)   97
   × 0.57

19)   14
   × 0.34

20)   29
   × 0.46

Multiplication, Decimals

Assignment 34

Name _____   Score _____

1) $\begin{array}{r} 427 \\ \times\ 0.7 \\ \hline \end{array}$ 2) $\begin{array}{r} 156 \\ \times\ 0.1 \\ \hline \end{array}$ 3) $\begin{array}{r} 778 \\ \times\ 0.4 \\ \hline \end{array}$ 4) $\begin{array}{r} 893 \\ \times\ 0.5 \\ \hline \end{array}$ 5) $\begin{array}{r} 312 \\ \times\ 0.2 \\ \hline \end{array}$

6) $\begin{array}{r} 235 \\ \times\ 0.3 \\ \hline \end{array}$ 7) $\begin{array}{r} 564 \\ \times\ 0.4 \\ \hline \end{array}$ 8) $\begin{array}{r} 892 \\ \times\ 0.8 \\ \hline \end{array}$ 9) $\begin{array}{r} 442 \\ \times\ 0.2 \\ \hline \end{array}$ 10) $\begin{array}{r} 153 \\ \times\ 0.6 \\ \hline \end{array}$

11) $\begin{array}{r} 278 \\ \times\ 0.81 \\ \hline \end{array}$ 12) $\begin{array}{r} 597 \\ \times\ 0.52 \\ \hline \end{array}$ 13) $\begin{array}{r} 815 \\ \times\ 0.95 \\ \hline \end{array}$ 14) $\begin{array}{r} 737 \\ \times\ 0.46 \\ \hline \end{array}$ 15) $\begin{array}{r} 644 \\ \times\ 0.74 \\ \hline \end{array}$

16) $\begin{array}{r} 429 \\ \times\ 0.57 \\ \hline \end{array}$ 17) $\begin{array}{r} 973 \\ \times\ 0.82 \\ \hline \end{array}$ 18) $\begin{array}{r} 524 \\ \times\ 0.39 \\ \hline \end{array}$ 19) $\begin{array}{r} 385 \\ \times\ 0.41 \\ \hline \end{array}$ 20) $\begin{array}{r} 737 \\ \times\ 0.32 \\ \hline \end{array}$

Multiplication, Decimals

Assignment 35

1) 8,753
   × 0.7

2) 2,497
   × 0.5

3) 6,184
   × 0.4

4) 3,894
   × 0.6

5) 1,569
   × 0.3

6) 7,424
   × 0.4

7) 4,274
   × 0.6

8) 5,649
   × 0.8

9) 9,393
   × 0.5

10) 2,548
    × 0.3

11) 1,384
    × 0.24

12) 4,567
    × 0.65

13) 6,648
    × 0.97

14) 8,724
    × 0.61

15) 5,819
    × 0.33

16) 3,973
    × 0.69

17) 6,057
    × 0.42

18) 9,147
    × 0.25

19) 1,284
    × 0.51

20) 2,343
    × 0.82

Assignment 36

Name _____   Score _____

1) 32
  × 0.4

2) 14
  × 0.6

3) 56
  × 0.7

4) 88
  × 0.9

5) 21
  × 0.8

6) 43
  × 0.2

7) 75
  × 0.7

8) 47
  × 0.1

9) 28
  × 0.9

10) 31
  × 0.8

11) 93
  × 0.35

12) 86
  × 0.46

13) 48
  × 0.24

14) 31
  × 0.17

15) 89
  × 0.35

16) 57
  × 0.39

17) 54
  × 0.68

18) 33
  × 0.46

19) 61
  × 0.57

20) 84
  × 0.24

21) 466
  × 0.8

22) 199
  × 0.6

23) 301
  × 0.2

24) 736
  × 0.8

25) 471
  × 0.5

26) 223
  × 0.3

27) 546
  × 0.8

28) 757
  × 0.5

29) 864
  × 0.7

30) 124
  × 0.4

31) 335
  × 0.52

32) 510
  × 0.45

33) 734
  × 0.73

34) 965
  × 0.87

35) 468
  × 0.63

36) 796
  × 0.41

37) 261
  × 0.79

38) 489
  × 0.46

39) 697
  × 0.63

40) 942
  × 0.31

41) 1,212
  × 0.8

42) 3,053
  × 0.7

43) 7,446
  × 0.9

44) 5,727
  × 0.5

45) 3,993
  × 0.2

46) 1,158
  × 0.4

47) 9,309
  × 0.2

48) 7,642
  × 0.6

49) 4,235
  × 0.5

50) 6,416
  × 0.8

51) 8,713
  × 0.35

52) 5,389
  × 0.57

53) 1,089
  × 0.74

54) 4,989
  × 0.42

55) 3,163
  × 0.92

56) 2,437
  × 0.24

57) 6,549
  × 0.45

58) 7,683
  × 0.69

59) 5,728
  × 0.78

60) 5,879
  × 0.53

Part 2
Division

Assignment 37

Name _____   Score _____

1) $3\overline{)84}$ 2) $4\overline{)48}$ 3) $9\overline{)72}$ 4) $5\overline{)75}$ 5) $6\overline{)12}$

6) $4\overline{)56}$ 7) $9\overline{)81}$ 8) $5\overline{)25}$ 9) $3\overline{)69}$ 10) $2\overline{)76}$

11) $2\overline{)74}$ 12) $6\overline{)66}$ 13) $2\overline{)98}$ 14) $5\overline{)20}$ 15) $5\overline{)85}$

16) $4\overline{)64}$ 17) $2\overline{)36}$ 18) $7\overline{)91}$ 19) $4\overline{)76}$ 20) $6\overline{)36}$

Assignment 38

1) $4\overline{)28}$ 2) $6\overline{)30}$ 3) $5\overline{)80}$ 4) $6\overline{)84}$ 5) $3\overline{)36}$

6) $4\overline{)68}$ 7) $3\overline{)27}$ 8) $9\overline{)99}$ 9) $3\overline{)81}$ 10) $2\overline{)66}$

11) $7\overline{)70}$ 12) $4\overline{)96}$ 13) $7\overline{)21}$ 14) $5\overline{)65}$ 15) $6\overline{)48}$

16) $4\overline{)24}$ 17) $4\overline{)72}$ 18) $3\overline{)87}$ 19) $4\overline{)88}$ 20) $5\overline{)75}$

Assignment 39

1) $3\overline{)75}$ 2) $4\overline{)52}$ 3) $6\overline{)18}$ 4) $5\overline{)90}$ 5) $2\overline{)56}$

6) $3\overline{)42}$ 7) $3\overline{)27}$ 8) $8\overline{)64}$ 9) $4\overline{)40}$ 10) $8\overline{)56}$

11) $4\overline{)84}$ 12) $6\overline{)66}$ 13) $7\overline{)35}$ 14) $6\overline{)24}$ 15) $3\overline{)48}$

16) $6\overline{)72}$ 17) $4\overline{)60}$ 18) $2\overline{)38}$ 19) $5\overline{)85}$ 20) $8\overline{)48}$

Division, 2 Digits ÷ 1 Digit (no remainder)

Assignment 40

Name _____   Score _____

1) $74 \div \rule{2em}{0.4pt} = 37$

2) $35 \div \rule{2em}{0.4pt} = 7$

3) $64 \div \rule{2em}{0.4pt} = 8$

4) $72 \div \rule{2em}{0.4pt} = 18$

5) $28 \div \rule{2em}{0.4pt} = 4$

6) $54 \div \rule{2em}{0.4pt} = 9$

7) $80 \div \rule{2em}{0.4pt} = 10$

8) $24 \div \rule{2em}{0.4pt} = 6$

9) $57 \div \rule{2em}{0.4pt} = 19$

10) $69 \div \rule{2em}{0.4pt} = 23$

11) $40 \div \rule{2em}{0.4pt} = 5$

12) $75 \div \rule{2em}{0.4pt} = 15$

13) $96 \div \rule{2em}{0.4pt} = 48$

14) $66 \div \rule{2em}{0.4pt} = 11$

15) $48 \div \rule{2em}{0.4pt} = 24$

16) $72 \div \rule{2em}{0.4pt} = 12$

17) $60 \div \rule{2em}{0.4pt} = 15$

18) $96 \div \rule{2em}{0.4pt} = 16$

19) $34 \div \rule{2em}{0.4pt} = 17$

20) $21 \div \rule{2em}{0.4pt} = 3$

Find the missing number, 2 Digits ÷ 1 Digit (no remainder)

Assignment 41

Name _____   Score _____

1) $6\overline{)24}$ 2) $5\overline{)45}$ 3) $7\overline{)91}$ 4) $2\overline{)46}$ 5) $9\overline{)18}$ 6) $2\overline{)34}$

7) $3\overline{)63}$ 8) $7\overline{)77}$ 9) $4\overline{)72}$ 10) $8\overline{)24}$ 11) $3\overline{)78}$ 12) $4\overline{)76}$

13) $4\overline{)84}$ 14) $7\overline{)35}$ 15) $2\overline{)92}$ 16) $9\overline{)63}$ 17) $6\overline{)60}$ 18) $9\overline{)54}$

19) $8\overline{)64}$ 20) $4\overline{)88}$ 21) $6\overline{)84}$ 22) $3\overline{)60}$ 23) $3\overline{)36}$ 24) $5\overline{)80}$

25) $4\overline{)96}$ 26) $5\overline{)75}$ 27) $2\overline{)50}$ 28) $3\overline{)90}$ 29) $7\overline{)84}$ 30) $4\overline{)12}$

31) $3\overline{)33}$ 32) $4\overline{)60}$ 33) $3\overline{)72}$ 34) $6\overline{)96}$ 35) $6\overline{)48}$ 36) $3\overline{)84}$

37) $7\overline{)63}$ 38) $5\overline{)85}$ 39) $3\overline{)96}$ 40) $6\overline{)42}$ 41) $3\overline{)39}$ 42) $6\overline{)36}$

Assignment 42

1) $4\overline{)73}$ 2) $5\overline{)37}$ 3) $9\overline{)61}$ 4) $5\overline{)54}$ 5) $6\overline{)31}$

6) $4\overline{)57}$ 7) $9\overline{)92}$ 8) $5\overline{)36}$ 9) $3\overline{)70}$ 10) $2\overline{)87}$

11) $7\overline{)85}$ 12) $8\overline{)77}$ 13) $2\overline{)65}$ 14) $5\overline{)33}$ 15) $4\overline{)74}$

16) $6\overline{)53}$ 17) $2\overline{)27}$ 18) $7\overline{)82}$ 19) $9\overline{)64}$ 20) $6\overline{)33}$

Division, 2 Digits ÷ 1 Digit (remainder)

Assignment 43

1) $6\overline{)56}$ 2) $8\overline{)60}$ 3) $3\overline{)40}$ 4) $7\overline{)32}$ 5) $5\overline{)72}$

6) $3\overline{)34}$ 7) $5\overline{)76}$ 8) $9\overline{)58}$ 9) $3\overline{)43}$ 10) $8\overline{)82}$

11) $7\overline{)74}$ 12) $4\overline{)49}$ 13) $8\overline{)57}$ 14) $3\overline{)86}$ 15) $6\overline{)62}$

16) $5\overline{)46}$ 17) $4\overline{)75}$ 18) $3\overline{)22}$ 19) $4\overline{)87}$ 20) $5\overline{)16}$

Division, 2 Digits ÷ 1 Digit (remainder)

Assignment 44

1) $3\overline{)64}$ 2) $5\overline{)41}$ 3) $7\overline{)27}$ 4) $9\overline{)80}$ 5) $4\overline{)45}$

6) $6\overline{)93}$ 7) $2\overline{)35}$ 8) $3\overline{)73}$ 9) $9\overline{)51}$ 10) $5\overline{)62}$

11) $3\overline{)13}$ 12) $6\overline{)76}$ 13) $9\overline{)48}$ 14) $6\overline{)35}$ 15) $8\overline{)98}$

16) $5\overline{)56}$ 17) $7\overline{)43}$ 18) $4\overline{)29}$ 19) $5\overline{)78}$ 20) $6\overline{)95}$

Division, 2 Digits ÷ 1 Digit (remainder)

Assignment 45

1) 6)35 2) 5)52 3) 7)81 4) 2)63 5) 9)74 6) 2)93

7) 4)42 8) 7)78 9) 5)64 10) 8)29 11) 3)97 12) 4)75

13) 4)54 14) 7)25 15) 3)82 16) 9)51 17) 6)40 18) 9)34

19) 8)55 20) 4)77 21) 6)37 22) 3)50 23) 4)86 24) 5)67

25) 4)43 26) 5)39 27) 2)65 28) 3)13 29) 7)94 30) 4)27

31) 3)34 32) 4)61 33) 3)73 34) 6)97 35) 8)47 36) 3)85

37) 7)62 38) 5)84 39) 3)95 40) 6)41 41) 8)23 42) 6)37

Division Timed Test, 2 Digits ÷ 1 Digit (remainder)

Assignment 46

Name _____   Score _____

1) $8 \overline{)824}$ 2) $3 \overline{)438}$ 3) $2 \overline{)712}$ 4) $5 \overline{)725}$ 5) $7 \overline{)182}$

6) $4 \overline{)596}$ 7) $8 \overline{)880}$ 8) $5 \overline{)375}$ 9) $3 \overline{)669}$ 10) $2 \overline{)756}$

11) $4 \overline{)744}$ 12) $6 \overline{)636}$ 13) $2 \overline{)928}$ 14) $5 \overline{)210}$ 15) $5 \overline{)805}$

16) $2 \overline{)694}$ 17) $4 \overline{)376}$ 18) $3 \overline{)951}$ 19) $8 \overline{)736}$ 20) $4 \overline{)316}$

Division, 3 Digits ÷ 1 Digit (no remainder)

Assignment 47

1) $4\overline{)128}$ 2) $6\overline{)330}$ 3) $5\overline{)580}$ 4) $8\overline{)784}$ 5) $3\overline{)936}$

6) $4\overline{)268}$ 7) $2\overline{)526}$ 8) $8\overline{)888}$ 9) $3\overline{)381}$ 10) $2\overline{)766}$

11) $5\overline{)710}$ 12) $4\overline{)936}$ 13) $9\overline{)252}$ 14) $5\overline{)675}$ 15) $6\overline{)498}$

16) $4\overline{)236}$ 17) $6\overline{)756}$ 18) $3\overline{)879}$ 19) $2\overline{)698}$ 20) $5\overline{)705}$

Division, 3 Digits ÷ 1 Digit (no remainder)

Assignment 48

1) $5\overline{)275}$ 2) $4\overline{)452}$ 3) $6\overline{)618}$ 4) $5\overline{)890}$ 5) $2\overline{)156}$

6) $3\overline{)342}$ 7) $3\overline{)627}$ 8) $2\overline{)964}$ 9) $4\overline{)240}$ 10) $8\overline{)552}$

11) $4\overline{)984}$ 12) $6\overline{)768}$ 13) $5\overline{)535}$ 14) $6\overline{)324}$ 15) $3\overline{)150}$

16) $6\overline{)276}$ 17) $4\overline{)660}$ 18) $2\overline{)938}$ 19) $5\overline{)485}$ 20) $8\overline{)744}$

Division, 3 Digits ÷ 1 Digit (no remainder)

Assignment 49

1) $374 \div \underline{\hspace{1cm}} = 187$

2) $535 \div \underline{\hspace{1cm}} = 107$

3) $464 \div \underline{\hspace{1cm}} = 58$

4) $772 \div \underline{\hspace{1cm}} = 193$

5) $828 \div \underline{\hspace{1cm}} = 138$

6) $534 \div \underline{\hspace{1cm}} = 89$

7) $810 \div \underline{\hspace{1cm}} = 90$

8) $244 \div \underline{\hspace{1cm}} = 61$

9) $528 \div \underline{\hspace{1cm}} = 66$

10) $675 \div \underline{\hspace{1cm}} = 75$

11) $336 \div \underline{\hspace{1cm}} = 56$

12) $745 \div \underline{\hspace{1cm}} = 149$

13) $956 \div \underline{\hspace{1cm}} = 478$

14) $678 \div \underline{\hspace{1cm}} = 113$

15) $488 \div \underline{\hspace{1cm}} = 244$

16) $792 \div \underline{\hspace{1cm}} = 132$

17) $810 \div \underline{\hspace{1cm}} = 270$

18) $938 \div \underline{\hspace{1cm}} = 134$

19) $354 \div \underline{\hspace{1cm}} = 177$

20) $272 \div \underline{\hspace{1cm}} = 34$

Assignment 50

Name _____   Score _____

1) $2\overline{)214}$ 2) $5\overline{)435}$ 3) $8\overline{)952}$ 4) $4\overline{)840}$ 5) $9\overline{)198}$ 6) $2\overline{)304}$

7) $7\overline{)532}$ 8) $3\overline{)747}$ 9) $6\overline{)762}$ 10) $4\overline{)284}$ 11) $3\overline{)738}$ 12) $4\overline{)756}$

13) $2\overline{)874}$ 14) $5\overline{)395}$ 15) $4\overline{)912}$ 16) $3\overline{)633}$ 17) $5\overline{)650}$ 18) $7\overline{)574}$

19) $8\overline{)624}$ 20) $4\overline{)832}$ 21) $6\overline{)744}$ 22) $2\overline{)650}$ 23) $3\overline{)366}$ 24) $5\overline{)870}$

25) $2\overline{)986}$ 26) $5\overline{)795}$ 27) $6\overline{)510}$ 28) $9\overline{)909}$ 29) $6\overline{)834}$ 30) $2\overline{)142}$

31) $3\overline{)363}$ 32) $4\overline{)608}$ 33) $3\overline{)792}$ 34) $6\overline{)924}$ 35) $2\overline{)446}$ 36) $3\overline{)864}$

37) $7\overline{)637}$ 38) $5\overline{)855}$ 39) $3\overline{)978}$ 40) $6\overline{)492}$ 41) $8\overline{)248}$ 42) $6\overline{)378}$

Division Timed Test, 3 Digits ÷ 1 Digit (no remainder)

Assignment 51

Name _____ Score _____

1) $4\overline{)273}$ 2) $5\overline{)437}$ 3) $9\overline{)561}$ 4) $5\overline{)754}$ 5) $6\overline{)131}$

6) $4\overline{)957}$ 7) $9\overline{)392}$ 8) $5\overline{)836}$ 9) $3\overline{)670}$ 10) $2\overline{)287}$

11) $7\overline{)485}$ 12) $8\overline{)577}$ 13) $2\overline{)765}$ 14) $5\overline{)146}$ 15) $4\overline{)974}$

16) $6\overline{)353}$ 17) $2\overline{)827}$ 18) $7\overline{)682}$ 19) $9\overline{)264}$ 20) $6\overline{)433}$

Division, 3 Digits ÷ 1 Digit (remainder)

Assignment 52

1) $6\overline{)856}$ 2) $8\overline{)561}$ 3) $3\overline{)244}$ 4) $7\overline{)932}$ 5) $5\overline{)672}$

6) $3\overline{)334}$ 7) $5\overline{)176}$ 8) $9\overline{)758}$ 9) $3\overline{)443}$ 10) $8\overline{)882}$

11) $7\overline{)575}$ 12) $4\overline{)249}$ 13) $8\overline{)957}$ 14) $3\overline{)686}$ 15) $6\overline{)362}$

16) $5\overline{)146}$ 17) $4\overline{)775}$ 18) $3\overline{)422}$ 19) $4\overline{)878}$ 20) $5\overline{)516}$

Division, 3 Digits ÷ 1 Digit (remainder)

Assignment 53

Name _____   Score _____

1) $3 \overline{)565}$ 2) $5 \overline{)641}$ 3) $7 \overline{)428}$ 4) $9 \overline{)780}$ 5) $4 \overline{)381}$

6) $6 \overline{)893}$ 7) $2 \overline{)235}$ 8) $3 \overline{)973}$ 9) $9 \overline{)151}$ 10) $5 \overline{)562}$

11) $3 \overline{)613}$ 12) $6 \overline{)476}$ 13) $9 \overline{)748}$ 14) $6 \overline{)335}$ 15) $8 \overline{)898}$

16) $5 \overline{)256}$ 17) $7 \overline{)943}$ 18) $4 \overline{)129}$ 19) $5 \overline{)578}$ 20) $6 \overline{)615}$

     Division, 3 Digits ÷ 1 Digit (remainder)

Assignment 54

Name _____ Score _____

1) 6)524 2) 8)645 3) 7)491 4) 3)746 5) 9)318 6) 2)825

7) 5)253 8) 7)977 9) 3)572 10) 9)624 11) 4)478 12) 3)776

13) 8)385 14) 7)835 15) 2)291 16) 8)963 17) 6)560 18) 9)654

19) 7)464 20) 6)788 21) 7)384 22) 3)860 23) 5)236 24) 4)981

25) 4)597 26) 5)677 27) 2)453 28) 3)790 29) 7)384 30) 5)812

31) 3)233 32) 4)963 33) 3)572 34) 6)697 35) 8)446 36) 3)784

37) 7)363 38) 9)885 39) 3)296 40) 5)942 41) 8)124 42) 6)536

Division Timed Test, 3 Digits ÷ 1 Digit (remainder)

Assignment 55

1) $3\overline{)2184}$ 2) $4\overline{)4348}$ 3) $2\overline{)6772}$ 4) $5\overline{)8175}$ 5) $4\overline{)1012}$

6) $6\overline{)3948}$ 7) $9\overline{)5283}$ 8) $5\overline{)7925}$ 9) $3\overline{)9267}$ 10) $2\overline{)4176}$

11) $2\overline{)5374}$ 12) $6\overline{)3264}$ 13) $2\overline{)6898}$ 14) $5\overline{)2720}$ 15) $8\overline{)7280}$

16) $4\overline{)1964}$ 17) $2\overline{)8936}$ 18) $7\overline{)5495}$ 19) $4\overline{)6976}$ 20) $6\overline{)3234}$

Assignment 56

1) $4\overline{)6328}$ 2) $6\overline{)3132}$ 3) $5\overline{)9280}$ 4) $6\overline{)5388}$ 5) $3\overline{)2238}$

6) $4\overline{)7968}$ 7) $3\overline{)1629}$ 8) $9\overline{)4095}$ 9) $3\overline{)8481}$ 10) $2\overline{)6956}$

11) $7\overline{)3570}$ 12) $4\overline{)9096}$ 13) $7\overline{)5222}$ 14) $5\overline{)2765}$ 15) $6\overline{)7344}$

16) $4\overline{)1424}$ 17) $4\overline{)4372}$ 18) $3\overline{)8988}$ 19) $4\overline{)6388}$ 20) $5\overline{)3475}$

Assignment 57

Name _____   Score _____

1) 3)9276   2) 4)7152   3) 6)5316   4) 5)3290   5) 7)1351

6) 3)4644   7) 3)6927   8) 8)8368   9) 4)2640   10) 8)9152

11) 4)7384   12) 6)5268   13) 7)3535   14) 6)1524   15) 3)4347

16) 6)6672   17) 4)8260   18) 2)2538   19) 5)9385   20) 8)7248

Division, 4 Digits ÷ 1 Digit (no remainder)

Assignment 58

Name _____ Score _____

1) $5{,}374 \div$ _____ $= 2{,}687$ 11) $7{,}931 \div$ _____ $= 1{,}133$

2) $7{,}235 \div$ _____ $= 1{,}447$ 12) $3{,}475 \div$ _____ $= 695$

3) $3{,}968 \div$ _____ $= 496$ 13) $9{,}296 \div$ _____ $= 4{,}648$

4) $9{,}072 \div$ _____ $= 2{,}268$ 14) $1{,}362 \div$ _____ $= 227$

5) $1{,}428 \div$ _____ $= 204$ 15) $6{,}948 \div$ _____ $= 3{,}474$

6) $6{,}354 \div$ _____ $= 1{,}059$ 16) $4{,}272 \div$ _____ $= 712$

7) $4{,}184 \div$ _____ $= 523$ 17) $8{,}680 \div$ _____ $= 2{,}170$

8) $8{,}924 \div$ _____ $= 2{,}231$ 18) $2{,}492 \div$ _____ $= 356$

9) $2{,}556 \div$ _____ $= 852$ 19) $5{,}134 \div$ _____ $= 2{,}567$

1 $5{,}268 \div$ _____ $= 1{,}756$ 20) $7{,}721 \div$ _____ $= 1{,}103$

  Find the missing number, 4 Digits ÷ 1 Digit (no remainder)

Assignment 59

Name _____   Score _____

1) 6)4620   2) 5)7245   3) 7)9394   4) 2)1546   5) 9)8613   6) 2)2434

7) 4)6956   8) 7)3675   9) 4)5872   10) 8)4328   11) 3)7176   12) 8)9272

13) 4)1784   14) 7)8533   15) 2)2092   16) 9)6561   17) 6)3762   18) 9)5355

19) 8)4264   20) 4)7688   21) 6)9288   22) 3)1560   23) 3)8235   24) 5)2780

25) 4)6796   26) 5)3475   27) 2)5250   28) 3)4890   29) 7)7686   30) 4)9612

31) 3)1434   32) 4)8760   33) 3)2574   34) 6)6972   35) 8)3848   36) 3)5985

37) 7)1764   38) 5)8685   39) 3)2496   40) 6)6942   41) 8)3128   42) 6)5634

Division Timed Test, 4 Digits ÷ 1 Digit (no remainder)

Assignment 60

Name _____   Score _____

1) 4)3183   2) 5)5347   3) 3)7771   4) 6)9175   5) 5)2011

6) 7)2946   7) 8)4282   8) 6)6925   9) 4)8266   10) 3)3175

11) 4)6373   12) 7)4265   13) 3)7897   14) 6)3721   15) 9)8282

16) 5)9963   17) 3)7934   18) 8)4493   19) 5)5977   20) 7)2235

    Division, 4 Digits ÷ 1 Digit (remainder)

Assignment 61

Name _____   Score _____

1) $5\overline{)5528}$ 2) $6\overline{)2032}$ 3) $7\overline{)8180}$ 4) $9\overline{)4288}$ 5) $3\overline{)1138}$

6) $5\overline{)6868}$ 7) $3\overline{)2729}$ 8) $8\overline{)3195}$ 9) $9\overline{)7381}$ 10) $4\overline{)5857}$

11) $7\overline{)2470}$ 12) $5\overline{)8196}$ 13) $8\overline{)4122}$ 14) $5\overline{)1664}$ 15) $6\overline{)6244}$

16) $9\overline{)2524}$ 17) $7\overline{)3272}$ 18) $3\overline{)7688}$ 19) $5\overline{)5263}$ 20) $2\overline{)2375}$

Division, 4 Digits ÷ 1 Digit (remainder)

Assignment 62

Name _____   Score _____

1) $5\overline{)8176}$ 2) $3\overline{)6052}$ 3) $6\overline{)4216}$ 4) $5\overline{)2191}$ 5) $7\overline{)7851}$

6) $3\overline{)3544}$ 7) $3\overline{)5827}$ 8) $8\overline{)7268}$ 9) $6\overline{)1540}$ 10) $8\overline{)8052}$

11) $9\overline{)6284}$ 12) $6\overline{)4168}$ 13) $7\overline{)2435}$ 14) $6\overline{)9424}$ 15) $3\overline{)3247}$

16) $6\overline{)5572}$ 17) $9\overline{)7160}$ 18) $3\overline{)1438}$ 19) $5\overline{)8286}$ 20) $8\overline{)6148}$

Division, 4 Digits ÷ 1 Digit (remainder)

Assignment 63

Name _____   Score _____

1) 6)4935   2) 5)6252   3) 7)7181   4) 2)2463   5) 9)5574   6) 2)8093

7) 4)1742   8) 7)3978   9) 5)9164   10) 8)4529   11) 3)6896   12) 4)7275

13) 4)2954   14) 7)5325   15) 3)8782   16) 9)1551   17) 6)3640   18) 9)9734

19) 8)4255   20) 4)6877   21) 6)7043   22) 3)2150   23) 4)5486   24) 5)8062

25) 4)1743   26) 5)3839   27) 2)9965   28) 3)4013   29) 7)6294   30) 4)7527

31) 3)2035   32) 4)5361   33) 3)8972   34) 6)1497   35) 8)3871   36) 3)9185

37) 7)4162   38) 5)6884   39) 3)7295   40) 6)2841   41) 8)5923   42) 6)8037

Assignment 64

Name _____   Score _____

1) 94)284   2) 74)548   3) 59)872   4) 35)176   5) 16)412

6) 84)656   7) 69)481   8) 45)325   9) 23)769   10) 92)277

11) 73)574   12) 56)866   13) 32)198   14) 15)421   15) 84)685

16) 62)464   17) 42)337   18) 27)791   19) 94)276   20) 76)536

Division, 3 Digits ÷ 2 Digits (remainder)

Assignment 65

1) $34\overline{)528}$ 2) $56\overline{)730}$ 3) $85\overline{)180}$ 4) $26\overline{)984}$ 5) $13\overline{)436}$

6) $94\overline{)368}$ 7) $43\overline{)227}$ 8) $64\overline{)699}$ 9) $73\overline{)808}$ 10) $32\overline{)567}$

11) $57\overline{)770}$ 12) $84\overline{)196}$ 13) $27\overline{)921}$ 14) $15\overline{)468}$ 15) $96\overline{)348}$

16) $41\overline{)254}$ 17) $64\overline{)672}$ 18) $75\overline{)887}$ 19) $34\overline{)513}$ 20) $55\overline{)725}$

Division, 3 Digits ÷ 2 Digits (remainder)

Assignment 66

Name _____   Score _____

1) $43\overline{)575}$ 2) $61\overline{)895}$ 3) $86\overline{)218}$ 4) $95\overline{)490}$ 5) $12\overline{)356}$

6) $33\overline{)942}$ 7) $25\overline{)127}$ 8) $58\overline{)664}$ 9) $73\overline{)740}$ 10) $48\overline{)556}$

11) $63\overline{)848}$ 12) $85\overline{)266}$ 13) $97\overline{)435}$ 14) $16\overline{)324}$ 15) $36\overline{)948}$

16) $26\overline{)173}$ 17) $54\overline{)660}$ 18) $72\overline{)738}$ 19) $46\overline{)585}$ 20) $68\overline{)831}$

Division, 3 Digits ÷ 2 Digits (remainder)

Assignment 67

1) 26)835   2) 45)552   3) 67)481   4) 92)163   5) 59)774   6) 12)693

7) 34)242   8) 87)978   9) 75)364   10) 28)829   11) 43)597   12) 64)475

13) 94)154   14) 57)725   15) 13)682   16) 39)251   17) 86)940   18) 79)334

19) 28)855   20) 44)568   21) 63)424   22) 93)150   23) 54)786   24) 15)621

25) 34)243   26) 85)939   27) 72)365   28) 23)813   29) 47)594   30) 64)427

31) 43)182   32) 64)761   33) 98)673   34) 56)297   35) 18)947   36) 33)385

37) 81)862   38) 79)584   39) 23)495   40) 46)141   41) 61)723   42) 96)637

Assignment 68

Name _____   Score _____

1) $34\overline{)2473}$ 2) $65\overline{)5137}$ 3) $89\overline{)7961}$ 4) $15\overline{)4054}$ 5) $96\overline{)8731}$

6) $24\overline{)1457}$ 7) $59\overline{)3692}$ 8) $75\overline{)9436}$ 9) $43\overline{)2270}$ 10) $32\overline{)5987}$

11) $67\overline{)7585}$ 12) $82\overline{)4377}$ 13) $12\overline{)8265}$ 14) $95\overline{)1833}$ 15) $27\overline{)3474}$

16) $56\overline{)9253}$ 17) $72\overline{)2427}$ 18) $47\overline{)5682}$ 19) $39\overline{)7264}$ 20) $64\overline{)4917}$

Division, 4 Digits ÷ 2 Digits (remainder)

Assignment 69

1) $86\overline{)4156}$ 2) $38\overline{)6093}$ 3) $53\overline{)9340}$ 4) $97\overline{)1732}$ 5) $25\overline{)2572}$

6) $43\overline{)8634}$ 7) $75\overline{)3476}$ 8) $19\overline{)5958}$ 9) $63\overline{)7043}$ 10) $88\overline{)4682}$

11) $37\overline{)6274}$ 12) $54\overline{)9349}$ 13) $98\overline{)1657}$ 14) $23\overline{)2386}$ 15) $63\overline{)8562}$

16) $85\overline{)3946}$ 17) $34\overline{)5675}$ 18) $53\overline{)7922}$ 19) $94\overline{)4187}$ 20) $25\overline{)6716}$

Division, 4 Digits ÷ 2 Digits (remainder)

Assignment 70

1) $83\overline{)5364}$ 2) $45\overline{)7241}$ 3) $26\overline{)3127}$ 4) $79\overline{)9380}$ 5) $94\overline{)4145}$

6) $36\overline{)8693}$ 7) $52\overline{)1535}$ 8) $13\overline{)6473}$ 9) $69\overline{)2951}$ 10) $85\overline{)5162}$

11) $43\overline{)7513}$ 12) $26\overline{)3976}$ 13) $79\overline{)9248}$ 14) $96\overline{)4435}$ 15) $37\overline{)8598}$

16) $55\overline{)1256}$ 17) $16\overline{)6545}$ 18) $64\overline{)2829}$ 19) $85\overline{)5278}$ 20) $46\overline{)7095}$

Assignment 71

Name _____   Score _____

1) $26\overline{)5835}$ 2) $65\overline{)1052}$ 3) $97\overline{)2181}$ 4) $31\overline{)3263}$ 5) $17\overline{)8474}$ 6) $42\overline{)4693}$

7) $54\overline{)5942}$ 8) $87\overline{)7478}$ 9) $75\overline{)6864}$ 10) $28\overline{)9329}$ 11) $63\overline{)5297}$ 12) $94\overline{)1375}$

13) $34\overline{)2752}$ 14) $17\overline{)3725}$ 15) $42\overline{)8544}$ 16) $59\overline{)4051}$ 17) $86\overline{)5140}$ 18) $79\overline{)7834}$

19) $28\overline{)6553}$ 20) $64\overline{)9877}$ 21) $96\overline{)1744}$ 22) $33\overline{)2450}$ 23) $14\overline{)3886}$ 24) $45\overline{)8066}$

25) $57\overline{)4243}$ 26) $85\overline{)5639}$ 27) $72\overline{)7965}$ 28) $23\overline{)6213}$ 29) $67\overline{)9694}$ 30) $94\overline{)1727}$

31) $33\overline{)2534}$ 32) $14\overline{)3361}$ 33) $43\overline{)8273}$ 34) $56\overline{)4597}$ 35) $88\overline{)7147}$ 36) $73\overline{)6985}$

37) $67\overline{)9562}$ 38) $95\overline{)1384}$ 39) $38\overline{)2995}$ 40) $16\overline{)3041}$ 41) $48\overline{)8623}$ 42) $56\overline{)4537}$

Division Timed Test, 4 Digits ÷ 2 Digits (remainder)

Assignment 72

1) $0.5 \div 10 =$ _____

2) $0.2 \div 100 =$ _____

3) $0.8 \div 1000 =$ _____

4) $0.6 \div 100 =$ _____

5) $0.9 \div 10 =$ _____

6) $0.8 \div 1000 =$ _____

7) $0.7 \div 10 =$ _____

8) $0.5 \div 100 =$ _____

9) $0.3 \div 10 =$ _____

10) $0.2 \div 1000 =$ _____

11) $0.62 \div 1000 =$ _____

12) $0.47 \div 10 =$ _____

13) $0.32 \div 1000 =$ _____

14) $0.45 \div 100 =$ _____

15) $0.87 \div 10 =$ _____

16) $0.73 \div 1000 =$ _____

17) $0.92 \div 100 =$ _____

18) $0.57 \div 10 =$ _____

19) $0.34 \div 100 =$ _____

20) $0.46 \div 1000 =$ _____

Division, Decimals

Assignment 73

1) $1.7 \div 100 =$ _____

2) $3.1 \div 10 =$ _____

3) $4.4 \div 1000 =$ _____

4) $6.5 \div 100 =$ _____

5) $9.2 \div 10 =$ _____

6) $4.3 \div 1000 =$ _____

7) $5.2 \div 100 =$ _____

8) $8.1 \div 10 =$ _____

9) $2.3 \div 100 =$ _____

10) $6.2 \div 1000 =$ _____

11) $8.21 \div 10 =$ _____

12) $5.17 \div 100 =$ _____

13) $9.53 \div 1000 =$ _____

14) $4.65 \div 100 =$ _____

15) $7.49 \div 10 =$ _____

16) $5.73 \div 1000 =$ _____

17) $8.27 \div 10 =$ _____

18) $3.89 \div 100 =$ _____

19) $4.12 \div 10 =$ _____

20) $3.25 \div 1000 =$ _____

Assignment 74

Name _____   Score _____

1) $23.7 \div 1000 =$ _____

2) $51.9 \div 10000 =$ _____

3) $46.3 \div 100 =$ _____

4) $12.6 \div 10000 =$ _____

5) $98.3 \div 1000 =$ _____

6) $63.9 \div 100 =$ _____

7) $38.7 \div 10000 =$ _____

8) $81.9 \div 1000 =$ _____

9) $27.4 \div 10000 =$ _____

10 $52.7 \div 100 =$ _____

11) $74.91 \div 1000 =$ _____

12) $65.37 \div 10000 =$ _____

13) $42.18 \div 1000 =$ _____

14) $14.67 \div 100 =$ _____

15) $95.21 \div 10000 =$ _____

16) $68.22 \div 100 =$ _____

17) $36.22 \div 1000 =$ _____

18) $47.82 \div 10000 =$ _____

19) $29.15 \div 100 =$ _____

20) $53.26 \div 1000 =$ _____

Division, Decimals

Assignment 75

Name _____ Score _____

1) $0.4 \div 100$

2) $0.6 \div 10$

3) $0.9 \div 1000$

4) $0.5 \div 100$

5) $0.3 \div 10$

6) $0.9 \div 1000$

7) $0.8 \div 10$

8) $0.2 \div 100$

9) $0.4 \div 10$

10) $0.6 \div 1000$

11) $0.58 \div 1000$

12) $0.35 \div 10$

13) $0.21 \div 1000$

14) $0.58 \div 100$

15) $0.76 \div 10$

16) $0.68 \div 1000$

17) $0.82 \div 100$

18) $0.93 \div 10$

19) $0.42 \div 100$

20) $0.57 \div 1000$

21) $3.8 \div 100$

22) $4.1 \div 10$

23) $5.5 \div 1000$

24) $7.1 \div 100$

25) $6.8 \div 10$

26) $2.7 \div 1000$

27) $9.5 \div 100$

28) $4.3 \div 10$

29) $3.1 \div 100$

30) $5.6 \div 1000$

31) $6.54 \div 10$

32) $3.28 \div 100$

33) $7.46 \div 1000$

34) $9.21 \div 100$

35) $8.35 \div 10$

36) $5.17 \div 1000$

37) $4.28 \div 10$

38) $1.36 \div 100$

39) $6.39 \div 10$

40) $3.17 \div 1000$

41) $46.1 \div 1000$

42) $57.2 \div 10000$

43) $92.4 \div 100$

44) $62.9 \div 10000$

45) $33.7 \div 1000$

46) $14.8 \div 100$

47) $26.4 \div 10000$

48) $74.9 \div 1000$

49) $86.2 \div 10000$

50) $44.5 \div 100$

51) $83.12 \div 1000$

52) $47.35 \div 10000$

53) $58.11 \div 1000$

54) $36.44 \div 100$

55) $74.93 \div 10000$

56) $18.27 \div 100$

57) $28.66 \div 1000$

58) $61.54 \div 10000$

59) $85.88 \div 100$

60) $42.18 \div 1000$

Answer Keys

Assignment 1

1) 54	11) 6
2) 21	12) 48
3) 72	13) 45
4) 25	14) 10
5) 12	15) 28
6) 36	16) 12
7) 27	17) 6
8) 30	18) 49
9) 8	19) 20
10) 18	20) 16

Assignment 2

1) 14	11) 63
2) 48	12) 32
3) 40	13) 49
4) 18	14) 0
5) 2	15) 30
6) 5	16) 12
7) 20	17) 8
8) 18	18) 6
9) 4	19) 28
10) 21	20) 24

Assignment 3

1) 15	11) 10
2) 9	12) 36
3) 48	13) 72
4) 54	14) 24
5) 6	15) 27
6) 8	16) 3
7) 35	17) 42
8) 28	18) 16
9) 36	19) 45
10) 6	20) 56

Assignment 4

1) 7	11) 3
2) 1	12) 7
3) 5	13) 9
4) 2	14) 3
5) 3	15) 4
6) 5	16) 5
7) 8	17) 8
8) 6	18) 4
9) 3	19) 3
10) 2	20) 7

Assignment 5

1) 28	11) 40	21) 3	31) 10	41) 54	51) 24
2) 9	12) 36	22) 0	32) 64	42) 20	52) 14
3) 56	13) 72	23) 28	33) 18	43) 24	53) 36
4) 36	14) 42	24) 15	34) 4	44) 12	54) 0
5) 6	15) 4	25) 7	35) 35	45) 81	55) 45
6) 24	16) 12	26) 12	36) 32	46) 18	56) 6
7) 45	17) 63	27) 54	37) 16	47) 5	57) 27
8) 2	18) 35	28) 49	38) 3	48) 32	58) 30
9) 0	19) 48	29) 8	39) 20	49) 8	59) 12
10) 24	20) 18	30) 9	40) 21	50) 25	60) 16

Assignment 6

1) 255	11) 66
2) 188	12) 408
3) 612	13) 297
4) 375	14) 105
5) 72	15) 315
6) 236	16) 192
7) 657	17) 72
8) 130	18) 679
9) 204	19) 60
10) 158	20) 174

Assignment 7

1) 54	11) 553
2) 448	12) 392
3) 390	13) 119
4) 558	14) 114
5) 36	15) 270
6) 140	16) 92
7) 320	17) 568
8) 828	18) 78
9) 42	19) 348
10) 371	20) 114

Assignment 8

1) 225	11) 680
2) 196	12) 396
3) 108	13) 432
4) 445	14) 144
5) 112	15) 57
6) 126	16) 438
7) 135	17) 228
8) 448	18) 70
9) 156	19) 420
10) 108	20) 344

Assignment 9

1) 2	11) 7
2) 5	12) 5
3) 8	13) 2
4) 4	14) 6
5) 7	15) 2
6) 6	16) 6
7) 8	17) 4
8) 4	18) 7
9) 3	19) 2
10) 3	20) 3

Assignment 10

1) 144	11) 102	21) 270	31) 165	41) 168	51) 213
2) 215	12) 252	22) 152	32) 204	42) 280	52) 190
3) 536	13) 336	23) 62	33) 219	43) 396	53) 126
4) 405	14) 112	24) 608	34) 384	44) 648	54) 392
5) 153	15) 0	25) 235	35) 322	45) 186	55) 585
6) 64	16) 702	26) 66	36) 474	46) 60	56) 74
7) 53	17) 468	27) 432	37) 427	47) 78	57) 432
8) 518	18) 216	28) 375	38) 425	48) 384	58) 332
9) 801	19) 434	29) 602	39) 291	49) 115	59) 252
10) 88	20) 352	30) 48	40) 252	50) 328	60) 342

Assignment 11

1) 925	11) 866
2) 694	12) 2,208
3) 4,544	13) 1,598
4) 4,650	14) 2,605
5) 7,308	15) 4,515
6) 1,036	16) 2,892
7) 3,311	17) 1,272
8) 3,130	18) 2,779
9) 2,904	19) 460
10) 358	20) 4,974

Assignment 12

1) 3,416	11) 1,953
2) 312	12) 2,392
3) 3,890	13) 5,719
4) 5,358	14) 2,214
5) 936	15) 3,870
6) 940	16) 1,692
7) 2,820	17) 7,768
8) 8,028	18) 1,578
9) 442	19) 1,548
10) 1,071	20) 2,214

Assignment 13

1) 5,250	11) 370
2) 996	12) 2,796
3) 1,854	13) 5,832
4) 1,945	14) 4,944
5) 312	15) 1,557
6) 2,226	16) 2,238
7) 2,135	17) 3,942
8) 3,948	18) 1,896
9) 3,756	19) 920
10) 508	20) 1,944

Assignment 14

1) 2	11) 3
2) 8	12) 7
3) 6	13) 9
4) 4	14) 3
5) 5	15) 4
6) 5	16) 5
7) 8	17) 8
8) 6	18) 4
9) 3	19) 6
10) 2	20) 7

Assignment 15

1) 1,620	11) 2,802	21) 3,720	31) 1,675	41) 968	51) 2,613
2) 858	12) 3,452	22) 1,194	32) 2,040	42) 2,440	52) 2,690
3) 3,976	13) 1,936	23) 602	33) 2,202	43) 6,696	53) 756
4) 7,929	14) 2,212	24) 5,888	34) 6,755	44) 5,148	54) 1,992
5) 1,953	15) 1,784	25) 2,350	35) 1,872	45) 786	55) 3,285
6) 864	16) 5,202	26) 669	36) 4,776	46) 460	56) 474
7) 5,271	17) 4,878	27) 4,368	37) 1,827	47) 1,878	57) 2,592
8) 474	18) 2,016	28) 3,790	38) 1,940	48) 4,584	58) 7,047
9) 2,601	19) 4,284	29) 6,048	39) 4,182	49) 2,115	59) 4,752
10) 2,488	20) 3,392	30) 496	40) 2,826	50) 5,128	60) 5,682

Assignment 16

1) 12,465	11) 52,031
2) 32,082	12) 16,340
3) 37,496	13) 15,898
4) 14,150	14) 27,126
5) 41,060	15) 3,290
6) 4,318	16) 59,784
7) 10,419	17) 18,544
8) 32,630	18) 16,779
9) 67,256	19) 6,230
10) 16,716	20) 24,087

Assignment 17

1) 7,281	11) 37,674
2) 18,936	12) 25,794
3) 35,390	13) 33,719
4) 16,986	14) 28,952
5) 42,496	15) 11,515
6) 8,645	16) 7,269
7) 5,164	17) 38,804
8) 74,628	18) 16,278
9) 21,710	19) 26,296
10) 12,612	20) 36,915

Assignment 18

1) 3,750	11) 5,550
2) 21,245	12) 27,936
3) 18,549	13) 56,232
4) 15,236	14) 41,210
5) 54,936	15) 10,638
6) 14,484	16) 27,784
7) 17,100	17) 32,880
8) 38,948	18) 18,496
9) 44,695	19) 29,288
10) 7,602	20) 7,494

Assignment 19

1) 5	11) 4
2) 4	12) 3
3) 6	13) 9
4) 8	14) 7
5) 2	15) 3
6) 2	16) 7
7) 3	17) 3
8) 6	18) 4
9) 8	19) 8
10) 5	20) 5

Assignment 20

1) 10,648	11) 9,326	21) 14,790	31) 44,010	41) 16,484	51) 42,355
2) 25,144	12) 56,441	22) 57,592	32) 20,416	42) 21,406	52) 4,614
3) 14,112	13) 26,304	23) 12,076	33) 47,138	43) 16,464	53) 72,864
4) 62,867	14) 65,844	24) 61,152	34) 27,795	44) 10,744	54) 27,490
5) 12,642	15) 62,454	25) 18,680	35) 18,720	45) 33,572	55) 50,190
6) 20,790	16) 11,956	26) 22,561	36) 43,980	46) 18,230	56) 50,659
7) 29,012	17) 45,794	27) 47,730	37) 10,088	47) 27,573	57) 41,832
8) 13,722	18) 12,944	28) 60,696	38) 24,265	48) 68,778	58) 7,132
9) 66,312	19) 49,032	29) 20,592	39) 20,091	49) 17,292	59) 10,416
10) 47,799	20) 16,696	30) 25,620	40) 35,652	50) 44,877	60) 32,283

Assignment 21

1) 276	11) 3,240
2) 2,516	12) 1,386
3) 4,012	13) 3,136
4) 3,525	14) 1,700
5) 8,160	15) 3,201
6) 6,636	16) 1,247
7) 3,332	17) 780
8) 390	18) 3,337
9) 3,869	19) 2,304
10) 2,478	20) 1,485

Assignment 22

1) 504	11) 2,565
2) 6,324	12) 532
3) 5,070	13) 1,479
4) 1,456	14) 6,174
5) 1,431	15) 3,634
6) 3,392	16) 912
7) 3,150	17) 4,176
8) 3,588	18) 1,378
9) 1,344	19) 6,674
10) 1,645	20) 1,679

Assignment 23

1) 2,184	11) 418
2) 3,738	12) 1,512
3) 1,134	13) 4,560
4) 2,499	14) 1,716
5) 2,025	15) 3,230
6) 1,944	16) 2,752
7) 2,184	17) 2,184
8) 5,056	18) 420
9) 1,107	19) 3,363
10) 513	20) 5,913

Assignment 24

1) 1,952	11) 2,590	21) 1,235	31) 2,765	41) 6,035	51) 2,394
2) 884	12) 2,491	22) 4,005	32) 1,104	42) 4,148	52) 6,035
3) 6,723	13) 1,548	23) 2,112	33) 1,248	43) 3,776	53) 1,517
4) 3,216	14) 4,108	24) 5,146	34) 6,132	44) 3,744	54) 1,242
5) 4,085	15) 1,170	25) 624	35) 2,397	45) 405	55) 4,503
6) 648	16) 3,588	26) 3,010	36) 1,848	46) 4,185	56) 1,456
7) 819	17) 1,504	27) 6,675	37) 2,485	47) 1,872	57) 5,727
8) 2,550	18) 5,208	28) 1,404	38) 1,092	48) 2,772	58) 2,256
9) 1,067	19) 2,052	29) 1,716	39) 1,470	49) 2,450	59) 3,367
10) 7,298	20) 1,333	30) 1,974	40) 4,462	50) 864	60) 1,040

Assignment 25

1) 8,835	11) 8,450
2) 21,850	12) 42,160
3) 67,228	13) 33,762
4) 38,709	14) 11,016
5) 7,875	15) 35,787
6) 26,865	16) 23,112
7) 66,794	17) 9,912
8) 10,918	18) 60,099
9) 26,182	19) 9,960
10) 17,468	20) 33,444

Assignment 26

1) 22,204	11) 12,933
2) 58,208	12) 19,072
3) 30,510	13) 50,149
4) 46,787	14) 36,354
5) 8,176	15) 33,542
6) 50,290	16) 9,541
7) 30,940	17) 58,302
8) 33,908	18) 9,205
9) 17,442	19) 56,256
10) 30,351	20) 13,545

Assignment 27

1) 25,568	11) 24,650
2) 20,874	12) 16,016
3) 12,627	13) 23,667
4) 42,068	14) 16,415
5) 15,201	15) 7,722
6) 16,692	16) 46,053
7) 6,775	17) 27,025
8) 30,221	18) 8,710
9) 18,170	19) 42,942
10) 21,112	20) 35,998

Assignment 28

1) 7,688	11) 9,424	21) 28,476	31) 17,877	41) 17,658	51) 26,492
2) 18,522	12) 21,488	22) 15,853	32) 22,016	42) 13,376	52) 22,892
3) 48,762	13) 45,576	23) 8,736	33) 23,488	43) 42,720	53) 14,058
4) 47,386	14) 48,664	24) 64,260	34) 47,432	44) 58,887	54) 42,226
5) 83,447	15) 11,726	25) 20,296	35) 33,726	45) 22,392	55) 61,275
6) 7,550	16) 30,498	26) 8,064	36) 51,610	46) 7,130	56) 10,152
7) 16,492	17) 49,780	27) 41,724	37) 48,048	47) 11,116	57) 44,408
8) 42,408	18) 48,336	28) 39,856	38) 43,809	48) 39,589	58) 35,776
9) 70,784	19) 70,684	29) 63,450	39) 33,048	49) 12,296	59) 27,264
10) 17,738	20) 8,162	30) 10,584	40) 32,300	50) 35,190	60) 35,774

Assignment 29

1) 76,475	11) 51,636
2) 226,044	12) 85,248
3) 512,304	13) 249,548
4) 351,900	14) 489,075
5) 70,668	15) 838,565
6) 175,986	16) 45,172
7) 724,881	17) 152,712
8) 73,170	18) 556,539
9) 495,344	19) 209,645
10) 192,759	20) 176,134

Assignment 30

1) 423,306	11) 151,767
2) 658,352	12) 269,145
3) 146,670	13) 621,224
4) 210,418	14) 228,997
5) 271,656	15) 413,376
6) 774,090	16) 79,352
7) 53,655	17) 806,096
8) 337,548	18) 184,240
9) 141,122	19) 186,048
10) 190,661	20) 223,944

Assignment 31

1) 551,376	11) 50,112
2) 117,265	12) 323,334
3) 241,098	13) 583,128
4) 428,562	14) 296,712
5) 192,276	15) 181,790
6) 239,666	16) 250,312
7) 251,082	17) 631,488
8) 412,085	18) 197,568
9) 409,596	19) 97,626
10) 63,525	20) 209,324

Assignment 32

1) 171,773	11) 289,819	21) 405,333	31) 184,305	41) 105,618	51) 296,242
2) 96,078	12) 388,440	22) 123,380	32) 234,738	42) 247,617	52) 296,395
3) 449,115	13) 201,664	23) 69,299	33) 271,728	43) 685,032	53) 81,675
4) 272,831	14) 224,857	24) 618,408	34) 762,824	44) 223,236	54) 209,412
5) 204,168	15) 187,383	25) 258,775	35) 201,283	45) 94,440	55) 354,341
6) 112,450	16) 532,128	26) 80,424	36) 509,568	46) 53,222	56) 57,000
7) 557,368	17) 504,897	27) 475,281	37) 203,970	47) 234,775	57) 317,814
8) 61,633	18) 215,424	28) 439,988	38) 237,944	48) 527,643	58) 759,995
9) 280,815	19) 459,525	29) 683,271	39) 425,658	49) 241,395	59) 364,734
10) 274,208	20) 390,218	30) 51,168	40) 329,770	50) 570,757	60) 364,188

Assignment 33

1) 42.5	11) 8.58
2) 9.4	12) 31.96
3) 54.4	13) 31.68
4) 45.6	14) 9.45
5) 10.8	15) 39.15
6) 9.6	16) 16.72
7) 32.9	17) 33.12
8) 30.5	18) 55.29
9) 28.8	19) 4.76
10) 3.4	20) 13.34

Assignment 34

1) 298.9	11) 225.18
2) 15.6	12) 310.44
3) 311.2	13) 774.25
4) 446.5	14) 339.02
5) 62.4	15) 476.56
6) 70.5	16) 244.53
7) 225.6	17) 797.86
8) 713.6	18) 204.36
9) 88.4	19) 157.85
10) 91.8	20) 235.84

Assignment 35

1) 6,127.1	11) 332.16
2) 1,248.5	12) 2,968.55
3) 2,473.6	13) 6,448.56
4) 2,336.4	14) 5,321.64
5) 470.7	15) 1,920.27
6) 2,969.6	16) 2,741.37
7) 2,564.4	17) 2,543.94
8) 4,519.2	18) 2,286.75
9) 4,696.5	19) 654.84
10) 764.4	20) 1,921.26

Assignment 36

1) 12.8	11) 32.55	21) 372.8	31) 174.2	41) 969.6	51) 3,049.55
2) 8.4	12) 39.56	22) 119.4	32) 229.5	42) 2,137.1	52) 3,071.73
3) 39.2	13) 11.52	23) 60.2	33) 535.82	43) 6,701.4	53) 805.86
4) 79.2	14) 5.27	24) 588.8	34) 839.55	44) 2,863.5	54) 2,095.38
5) 16.8	15) 31.15	25) 235.5	35) 294.84	45) 798.6	55) 2,909.96
6) 8.6	16) 22.23	26) 66.9	36) 326.36	46) 463.2	56) 584.88
7) 52.5	17) 36.72	27) 436.8	37) 206.19	47) 1,861.8	57) 2,947.05
8) 4.7	18) 15.18	28) 378.5	38) 224.94	48) 4,585.2	58) 5,301.27
9) 25.2	19) 34.77	29) 604.8	39) 439.11	49) 2,117.5	59) 4,467.84
10) 24.8	20) 20.16	30) 49.6	40) 292.02	50) 5,132.8	60) 3,115.87

Assignment 37

1) 28	11) 37
2) 12	12) 11
3) 8	13) 49
4) 15	14) 4
5) 2	15) 17
6) 14	16) 16
7) 9	17) 18
8) 5	18) 13
9) 23	19) 19
10) 38	20) 6

Assignment 38

1) 7	11) 10
2) 5	12) 24
3) 16	13) 3
4) 14	14) 13
5) 12	15) 8
6) 17	16) 6
7) 9	17) 18
8) 11	18) 29
9) 27	19) 22
10) 33	20) 15

Assignment 39

1) 25	11) 21
2) 13	12) 11
3) 3	13) 5
4) 18	14) 4
5) 28	15) 16
6) 14	16) 12
7) 9	17) 15
8) 8	18) 19
9) 10	19) 17
10) 7	20) 6

Assignment 40

1) 2	11) 8
2) 5	12) 5
3) 8	13) 2
4) 4	14) 6
5) 7	15) 2
6) 6	16) 6
7) 8	17) 4
8) 4	18) 6
9) 3	19) 2
10) 3	20) 7

Assignment 41

1) 4	8) 11	15) 46	22) 20	29) 12	36) 28
2) 9	9) 18	16) 7	23) 12	30) 3	37) 9
3) 13	10) 3	17) 10	24) 16	31) 11	38) 17
4) 23	11) 26	18) 6	25) 24	32) 15	39) 32
5) 2	12) 19	19) 8	26) 15	33) 24	40) 7
6) 17	13) 21	20) 22	27) 25	34) 16	41) 13
7) 21	14) 5	21) 14	28) 30	35) 8	42) 6

Assignment 42

1) 18 R1	11) 12 R1
2) 7 R2	12) 9 R5
3) 6 R7	13) 32 R1
4) 10 R4	14) 6 R3
5) 5 R1	15) 18 R2
6) 14 R1	16) 8 R5
7) 10 R2	17) 13 R1
8) 7 R1	18) 11 R5
9) 23 R1	19) 7 R1
10) 43 R1	20) 5 R3

Assignment 43

1) 9 R2	11) 10 R4
2) 7 R4	12) 12 R1
3) 13 R1	13) 7 R1
4) 4 R4	14) 28 R2
5) 14 R2	15) 10 R2
6) 11 R1	16) 9 R1
7) 15 R1	17) 18 R3
8) 6 R4	18) 7 R1
9) 14 R1	19) 21 R3
10) 10 R2	20) 3 R1

Assignment 44

1) 21 R1	11) 4 R1
2) 8 R1	12) 12 R4
3) 3 R6	13) 5 R3
4) 8 R8	14) 5 R5
5) 11 R1	15) 12 R2
6) 15 R3	16) 11 R1
7) 17 R1	17) 6 R1
8) 24 R1	18) 7 R1
9) 5 R6	19) 15 R3
10) 12 R2	20) 15 R5

Assignment 45

1) 5 R5	8) 11 R1	15) 27 R1	22) 16 R2	29) 13 R3	36) 28 R1
2) 10 R2	9) 12 R4	16) 5 R6	23) 21 R2	30) 6 R3	37) 8 R6
3) 11 R4	10) 3 R5	17) 6 R4	24) 13 R2	31) 11 R1	38) 16 R4
4) 31 R1	11) 32 R1	18) 3 R7	25) 10 R3	32) 15 R1	39) 31 R2
5) 8 R2	12) 18 R3	19) 6 R7	26) 7 R4	33) 24 R1	40) 6 R5
6) 46 R1	13) 13 R2	20) 19 R1	27) 32 R1	34) 16 R1	41) 2 R7
7) 10 R2	14) 3 R4	21) 6 R1	28) 4 R1	35) 5 R7	42) 6 R1

Assignment 46

1) 103	11) 186
2) 146	12) 106
3) 356	13) 464
4) 145	14) 42
5) 26	15) 161
6) 149	16) 347
7) 110	17) 94
8) 75	18) 317
9) 223	19) 92
10) 378	20) 79

Assignment 47

1) 32	11) 142
2) 55	12) 234
3) 116	13) 28
4) 98	14) 135
5) 312	15) 83
6) 67	16) 59
7) 263	17) 126
8) 111	18) 293
9) 127	19) 349
10) 383	20) 141

Assignment 48

1) 55	11) 246
2) 113	12) 128
3) 103	13) 107
4) 178	14) 54
5) 78	15) 50
6) 114	16) 46
7) 209	17) 165
8) 482	18) 469
9) 60	19) 97
10) 69	20) 93

Assignment 49

1) 2	11) 6
2) 5	12) 5
3) 8	13) 2
4) 4	14) 6
5) 6	15) 2
6) 6	16) 6
7) 9	17) 3
8) 4	18) 7
9) 8	19) 2
10) 9	20) 8

Assignment 50

1) 107	8) 249	15) 228	22) 325	29) 139	36) 288
2) 87	9) 127	16) 211	23) 122	30) 71	37) 91
3) 119	10) 71	17) 130	24) 174	31) 121	38) 171
4) 210	11) 246	18) 82	25) 493	32) 152	39) 326
5) 22	12) 189	19) 78	26) 159	33) 264	40) 82
6) 152	13) 437	20) 208	27) 85	34) 154	41) 31
7) 76	14) 79	21) 124	28) 101	35) 223	42) 63

Assignment 51

1) 68 R1	11) 69 R2
2) 87 R2	12) 72 R1
3) 62 R3	13) 382 R1
4) 150 R4	14) 29 R1
5) 21 R5	15) 243 R2
6) 239 R1	16) 58 R5
7) 43 R5	17) 413 R1
8) 167 R1	18) 97 R3
9) 233 R1	19) 29 R3
10) 143 R1	20) 72 R1

Assignment 52

1) 142 R4	11) 82 R1
2) 70 R1	12) 62 R1
3) 81 R1	13) 119 R5
4) 133 R1	14) 228 R2
5) 134 R2	15) 60 R2
6) 111 R1	16) 29 R1
7) 35 R1	17) 193 R3
8) 84 R2	18) 140 R2
9) 147 R2	19) 219 R2
10) 110 R2	20) 103 R1

Assignment 53

1) 188 R1	11) 204 R1
2) 128 R1	12) 79 R2
3) 61 R1	13) 83 R1
4) 86 R6	14) 55 R5
5) 95 R1	15) 112 R2
6) 148 R5	16) 51 R1
7) 117 R1	17) 134 R5
8) 324 R1	18) 32 R1
9) 16 R7	19) 115 R3
10) 112 R2	20) 102 R3

Assignment 54

1) 87 R2	8) 139 R4	15) 145 R1	22) 286 R2	29) 54 R6	36) 261 R1
2) 80 R5	9) 190 R2	16) 120 R3	23) 47 R1	30) 162 R2	37) 51 R6
3) 70 R1	10) 69 R3	17) 93 R2	24) 245 R1	31) 77 R2	38) 98 R3
4) 248 R2	11) 119 R2	18) 72 R6	25) 149 R1	32) 240 R3	39) 98 R2
5) 35 R3	12) 258 R2	19) 66 R2	26) 135 R2	33) 190 R2	40) 188 R2
6) 412 R1	13) 48 R1	20) 131 R2	27) 226 R1	34) 116 R1	41) 15 R4
7) 50 R3	14) 119 R2	21) 54 R6	28) 263 R1	35) 55 R6	42) 89 R2

Assignment 55

1) 728	11) 2,687
2) 1,087	12) 544
3) 3,386	13) 3,449
4) 1,635	14) 544
5) 253	15) 910
6) 658	16) 491
7) 587	17) 4,468
8) 1,585	18) 785
9) 3,089	19) 1,744
10) 2,088	20) 539

Assignment 56

1) 1,582	11) 510
2) 522	12) 2,274
3) 1,856	13) 746
4) 898	14) 553
5) 746	15) 1,224
6) 1,992	16) 356
7) 543	17) 1,093
8) 455	18) 2,996
9) 2,827	19) 1,597
10) 3,478	20) 695

Assignment 57

1) 3,092	11) 1,846
2) 1,788	12) 878
3) 886	13) 505
4) 658	14) 254
5) 193	15) 1,449
6) 1,548	16) 1,112
7) 2,309	17) 2,065
8) 1,046	18) 1,269
9) 660	19) 1,877
10) 1,144	20) 906

Assignment 58

1) 2	11) 7
2) 5	12) 5
3) 8	13) 2
4) 4	14) 6
5) 7	15) 2
6) 6	16) 6
7) 8	17) 4
8) 4	18) 7
9) 3	19) 2
10) 3	20) 7

Assignment 59

1) 770	8) 525	15) 1,046	22) 520	29) 1,098	36) 1,995
2) 1,449	9) 1,468	16) 729	23) 2,745	30) 2,403	37) 252
3) 1,342	10) 541	17) 627	24) 556	31) 478	38) 1,737
4) 773	11) 2,392	18) 595	25) 1,699	32) 2,190	39) 832
5) 957	12) 1,159	19) 533	26) 695	33) 858	40) 1,157
6) 1,217	13) 446	20) 1,922	27) 2,625	34) 1,162	41) 391
7) 1,739	14) 1,219	21) 1,548	28) 1,630	35) 481	42) 939

Assignment 60

1) 795 R3	11) 1,593 R1
2) 1,069 R2	12) 609 R2
3) 2,590 R1	13) 2,632 R1
4) 1,529 R1	14) 620 R1
5) 402 R1	15) 920 R2
6) 420 R6	16) 1,992 R3
7) 535 R2	17) 2,644 R2
8) 1,154 R1	18) 561 R5
9) 2,066 R2	19) 1,195 R2
10) 1,058 R1	20) 319 R2

Assignment 61

1) 1,105 R3	11) 352 R6
2) 338 R4	12) 1,639 R1
3) 1,168 R4	13) 515 R2
4) 476 R4	14) 332 R4
5) 379 R1	15) 1,040 R4
6) 1,373 R3	16) 280 R4
7) 909 R2	17) 467 R3
8) 399 R3	18) 2,562 R2
9) 820 R1	19) 1,052 R3
10) 1,464 R1	20) 1,187 R1

Assignment 62

1) 1,635 R1	11) 698 R2
2) 2,017 R1	12) 694 R4
3) 702 R4	13) 347 R6
4) 438 R1	14) 1,570 R4
5) 1,121 R4	15) 1,082 R1
6) 1,181 R1	16) 928 R4
7) 1,942 R1	17) 795 R5
8) 908 R4	18) 479 R1
9) 256 R4	19) 1,657 R1
10) 1,006 R4	20) 768 R4

Assignment 63

1) 822 R3	8) 568 R2	15) 2,927 R1	22) 716 R2	29) 899 R1	36) 3,061 R2
2) 1,250 R2	9) 1,832 R4	16) 172 R3	23) 1,371 R2	30) 1,881 R3	37) 594 R4
3) 1,025 R6	10) 566 R1	17) 606 R4	24) 1,612 R2	31) 678 R1	38) 1,376 R4
4) 1,231 R1	11) 2,298 R2	18) 1,081 R5	25) 435 R3	32) 1,340 R1	39) 2,431 R2
5) 619 R3	12) 1,818 R3	19) 531 R7	26) 767 R4	33) 2,990 R2	40) 473 R3
6) 4,046 R1	13) 738 R2	20) 1,719 R1	27) 4,982 R1	34) 249 R3	41) 740 R3
7) 435 R2	14) 760 R5	21) 1,173 R5	28) 1,337 R2	35) 483 R7	42) 1,339 R3

Assignment 64

1) 3 R2	11) 7 R63
2) 7 R30	12) 15 R26
3) 14 R46	13) 6 R6
4) 5 R1	14) 28 R1
5) 25 R12	15) 8 R13
6) 7 R68	16) 7 R30
7) 6 R67	17) 8 R1
8) 7 R10	18) 29 R8
9) 33 R10	19) 2 R88
10) 3 R1	20) 7 R4

Assignment 65

1) 15 R18	11) 13 R29
2) 13 R2	12) 2 R28
3) 2 R10	13) 34 R3
4) 37 R22	14) 31 R3
5) 33 R7	15) 3 R60
6) 3 R86	16) 6 R8
7) 5 R12	17) 10 R32
8) 10 R59	18) 11 R62
9) 11 R5	19) 15 R3
10) 17 R23	20) 13 R10

Assignment 66

1) 13 R16	11) 13 R29
2) 14 R41	12) 3 R11
3) 2 R46	13) 4 R47
4) 5 R15	14) 20 R4
5) 29 R8	15) 26 R12
6) 28 R18	16) 6 R17
7) 5 R2	17) 12 R12
8) 11 R26	18) 10 R18
9) 10 R10	19) 12 R33
10) 11 R28	20) 12 R15

Assignment 67

1) 32 R3	8) 11 R21	15) 52 R6	22) 1 R57	29) 12 R30	36) 11 R22
2) 12 R12	9) 4 R64	16) 6 R17	23) 14 R30	30) 6 R43	37) 10 R52
3) 7 R12	10) 29 R17	17) 10 R80	24) 41 R6	31) 4 R10	38) 7 R31
4) 1 R71	11) 13 R38	18) 4 R18	25) 7 R5	32) 11 R57	39) 21 R12
5) 13 R7	12) 7 R27	19) 30 R15	26) 11 R4	33) 6 R85	40) 3 R3
6) 57 R9	13) 1 R60	20) 12 R40	27) 5 R5	34) 5 R17	41) 11 R52
7) 7 R4	14) 12 R41	21) 6 R46	28) 35 R8	35) 52 R11	42) 6 R61

Assignment 68

1) 72 R25	11) 113 R14
2) 79 R2	12) 53 R31
3) 89 R40	13) 688 R9
4) 270 R4	14) 19 R28
5) 90 R91	15) 128 R18
6) 60 R17	16) 165 R13
7) 62 R34	17) 33 R51
8) 125 R61	18) 120 R42
9) 52 R34	19) 186 R10
10) 187 R3	20) 76 R53

Assignment 69

1) 48 R28	11) 169 R21
2) 160 R13	12) 173 R7
3) 176 R12	13) 16 R89
4) 17 R83	14) 103 R17
5) 102 R22	15) 135 R57
6) 200 R34	16) 46 R36
7) 46 R26	17) 166 R31
8) 313 R11	18) 149 R25
9) 111 R50	19) 44 R51
10) 53 R18	20) 268 R16

Assignment 70

1) 64 R52	11) 174 R31
2) 160 R41	12) 152 R24
3) 120 R7	13) 117 R5
4) 118 R58	14) 46 R19
5) 44 R9	15) 232 R14
6) 241 R17	16) 22 R46
7) 29 R27	17) 409 R1
8) 497 R12	18) 44 R13
9) 42 R53	19) 62 R8
10) 60 R62	20) 154 R11

Assignment 71

1) 224 R11	8) 85 R83	15) 203 R18	22) 74 R8	29) 144 R46	36) 95 R50
2) 16 R12	9) 91 R39	16) 68 R39	23) 277 R8	30) 18 R35	37) 142 R48
3) 22 R47	10) 333 R5	17) 59 R66	24) 179 R11	31) 76 R26	38) 14 R54
4) 105 R8	11) 84 R5	18) 99 R13	25) 74 R25	32) 240 R1	39) 78 R31
5) 498 R8	12) 14 R59	19) 234 R1	26) 66 R29	33) 192 R17	40) 190 R1
6) 111 R31	13) 80 R32	20) 154 R21	27) 110 R45	34) 82 R5	41) 179 R31
7) 110 R2	14) 219 R2	21) 18 R16	28) 270 R3	35) 81 R19	42) 81 R1

Assignment 72

1) 0.05	11) 0.00062
2) 0.002	12) 0.047
3) 0.0008	13) 0.00032
4) 0.006	14) 0.0045
5) 0.09	15) 0.087
6) 0.0008	16) 0.00073
7) 0.07	17) 0.0092
8) 0.005	18) 0.057
9) 0.03	19) 0.0034
10) 0.0002	20) 0.00046

Assignment 73

1) 0.017	11) 0.821
2) 0.31	12) 0.0517
3) 0.0044	13) 0.00953
4) 0.065	14) 0.0465
5) 0.92	15) 0.749
6) 0.0043	16) 0.00573
7) 0.052	17) 0.827
8) 0.81	18) 0.0389
9) 0.023	19) 0.412
10) 0.0062	20) 0.00325

Assignment 74

1) 0.0237	11) 0.07491
2) 0.00519	12) 0.006537
3) 0.463	13) 0.04218
4) 0.00126	14) 0.1467
5) 0.0983	15) 0.009521
6) 0.639	16) 0.6822
7) 0.00387	17) 0.03622
8) 0.0819	18) 0.004782
9) 0.00274	19) 0.2915
10) 0.527	20) 0.05326

Assignment 75

1) 0.004	11) 0.00058	21) 0.038	31) 0.654	41) 0.0461	51) 0.08312
2) 0.06	12) 0.035	22) 0.41	32) 0.0328	42) 0.00572	52) 0.004735
3) 0.0009	13) 0.00021	23) 0.0055	33) 0.00746	43) 0.924	53) 0.05811
4) 0.005	14) 0.0058	24) 0.071	34) 0.0921	44) 0.00629	54) 0.3644
5) 0.03	15) 0.076	25) 0.68	35) 0.835	45) 0.0337	55) 0.007493
6) 0.0009	16) 0.00068	26) 0.0027	36) 0.00517	46) 0.148	56) 0.1827
7) 0.08	17) 0.0082	27) 0.095	37) 0.428	47) 0.00264	57) 0.02866
8) 0.002	18) 0.093	28) 0.43	38) 0.0136	48) 0.0749	58) 0.006154
9) 0.04	19) 0.0042	29) 0.031	39) 0.639	49) 0.00862	59) 0.8588
10) 0.0006	20) 0.00057	30) 0.0056	40) 0.00317	50) 0.445	60) 0.04218

Made in the USA
Columbia, SC
20 July 2021